The Story of My Life

Written for my Children

Caroline Mackensen Romberg

Summer 1939

The Story of My Life
Written for my Children
Caroline Mackensen Romberg
Summer 1939

Compiled and edited by Annie Romberg 1970
Revised and reformatted by Kenneth W. Fuchs 2001
Edited by Stephen A. Engelking
ISBN: 978-3-949197-09-3

The publishers are most grateful for the material provided by Kenneth Fuchs, the work painstakingly carried
out by his family and the support he has given to this
project of preserving this valuable historic document.

Contents

The Romberg Connection

Caroline Mackensen married Julius Romberg who was the youngest son of the Texas-German poet Johannes Romberg.

Louise Fuchs née Romberg writes[1]:

My father, Johannes Romberg, was the only son and only child of a preacher, and as was customary at the time, he was to become a preacher but weak eyes, which he had contracted from a cold with measles, prevented him from studying. He had a great inclination to learn a trade, but in those days it was beneath rank and dignity for him to learn a trade as the son of a preacher, so he was destined to become a merchant. It turned out, however, that he had neither desire nor inclination to do so. Still very young, he was apprenticed to a merchant Bauch, whose second oldest daughter Friederike later became our mother. He was very shy and timid and my mother, herself still a child, felt pity for his abandonment. I don't know how it happened but they became good comrades. She read a lot to him in free hours and often they talked what they had read through together. He was a thinker and brooding man. She was destined to be a teacher and also became an extraordinarily clever woman who took on any well-educated German in debate. I still remember this clearly because in our American "settlement" there lived many educated, highly trained neighbors, from over there — preachers, officers, doctors, lawyers, and so on.

---

1   *Erinnerungen von Louise Fuchs geb Romberg. Niedergeschrieben im 84ten Jahr .* Translated here by the editor. The book *Reminiscences of Louise Romberg Fuchs 1927* translated from the German by Helen and Gertrude Franke 1936, renders her perspective of her adventures as a Texas pioneer.

At the age of fourteen Friederike became engaged to Johannes Romberg. Then she became a teacher and left the parental home. Only when she was 24 years old (1833) did the two get married. They lived in Boizenburg on the Elbe, where my father started his own business (1833).

Here four daughters and two sons were born—me in 1840. My father never went to his store with pleasure, and where he found an opportunity to do carpentry and masonry work in or at home, he did it. He was not fond of trade, he preferred writing poems. He also liked to keep himself busy in the garden. Later here in America, his mother had to take care of all business.

There is a strong connection between the Fuchs family—pioneers of Texas and the Rombergs. In Cat Spring the Fuchs family became close friends with the Rombergs, who had also settled there before moving to Fayette County. Caroline Romberg, daughter of Johannes Romberg the poet, married Pastor Adolf Fuchs' son Hermann. Her sister Louise Romberg married Wilhelm Fuchs, another son of Pastor Adolf.

Fuchs was also an associate of the famous poet von Hoffmann von Fallersleben[2]. Fuchs addressed this letter

---

2 August Heinrich Hoffmann von Fallersleben was a German poet, scholar, librettist, and author of Texas lyrics. He wrote the lyrics to *Lied der Deutschen*, aka. *Deutschlandlied*, a song that became one of the symbols of the March Revolution of 1848, the aftermath of which brought many immigrants to Texas. The song has since been adopted as the national anthem of Germany. He began an association with Texas in 1843 when he came in contact with Gustav Dresel, a German who had returned from spending four years in the Houston area as a merchant and cotton exporter. While working with Dresel on a journal of his experiences in Texas, Hoffmann also befriended Adolf Fuchs just a few weeks before the Fuchs family sailed for Texas in late 1845. For their departure Hoffmann wrote his first poem about the Lone Star emblem, *Der Stern von Texas*, now called the Texas German anthem. The two men began work on Dresel's Texas journal, which was published in Germany with the false statement on the title page saying it was written by Texas Germans and published in San Felipe by "Adolph Fuchs & Co.". It has been republished

to von Fallersleben, whom he had met shortly before leaving for Texas[3]:

Carl Adolf Friedrich Fuchs

Adolph Fuchs was a protestant clergyman at Koelzow in the Rostock area. For many years he filled the position of pastor to the satisfaction of his small congregation. His income was very limited, so that in the course of time he had to use up his own and his wife's means. Since he could not agree with the theological views of the church authorities, which were old-orthodox and bigoted, he could never expect any pecuniary improvement in his position. Therefore, he decided to emigrate and give his large family a better future and to find for himself a vocation more in agreement with his convictions. In the autumn of 1845 he said farewell to his congregation (his farewell sermon has been printed), boarded a sailing ship in Bremen and, around Christmas time of

as *Gustav Dresel's Houston Journal*, (Austin: University of Texas Press, 1954).

Hoffmann completed his collection of thirty-one Texas songs, *Texanische Lieder*, in 1846. In order to circumvent censorship regulations, Hoffmann had the title page state that the book was written by German Texans and published in San Felipe, Texas, by "Adolf Fuchs & Co.," whereas it actually came out in Wandsbeck, Germany.

(Dresel, Gustav. *The Handbook of Texas Online*, Texas State Historical Association (TSHA). *Tshaonlineorg*. 2017. Available at: https://tshaonline.org/handbook/online/articles/fdr02. Accessed September 7, 2017.; Deutschlandlied. *Enwikipediaorg*. 2017. Available at: https://en.wikipedia.org/wiki/Deutschlandlied. Accessed September 7, 2017..)

3   Sourced from: Woodrick, James V. and Engelking Stephen A. (2017), Cat Spring Pioneers — German Immigrants Building a New Life in Texas, Texianer Verlag.

the same year, he and his loved ones landed safely in Galveston. He is a man of sterling character, full of determination, energy and endurance, and yet a charming personality, endowed by nature with these most precious talents: He teaches, preaches, writes, speaks several languages, does wood-turning and carpentry, knows about agriculture and gardening, plays the violin, piano and guitar, and is outstanding as a singer.

In *The Millheim and Cat Spring Pioneers*[4] cited above we read:

Carl Adolf Friedrich Fuchs was from Mecklenburg, in northern Germany. As a youth he enjoyed outdoor activities and he learned to play the violin. He entered university at the age of eighteen and studied theology and philosophy at the Universities of Halle, Berlin, Rostock, and Jena. He married Luise Rumker in 1829, and for the next six years taught school in Waren. He became pastor at the Lutheran church in Kolzow in 1835, and preached there for ten years. He became interested in emigration to North America, and in 1836 he published a poem called "The New Fatherland." During this time he also wrote a novel dealing with a young theological student-minister who eventually became very critical of the conditions of the Evangelical Church in Germany in the 1830s and decided to emigrate to North America. The novel *Robert* was published in Rostock in 1842.

In 1844 he obtained a certificate for a quarter-league of land (1,107 acres) on the Colorado river in Texas that had initially been awarded to a participant in the Texas Revolution, and later sold. Fuchs became disenchanted with the strict orthodoxy then being practiced by church authorities, and had begun receiving criticism for the views he expressed in his novel. He applied to emigrate

---

4   Ibid. p. 84.

to Texas under the auspices of the Adelsverein, and finally was given room on a ship that left in 1845. Fuchs
gave up his ministry when he left Germany. When they
arrived in Galveston they learned of a fever epidemic in
Indianola, their intended destination, so they debarked
at Galveston and made their way to Cat Spring. They
bought a farm which provided most of their sustenance;
Fuchs also taught school in a new schoolhouse/commu-
nity center, and taught music at the Institute for Young
Ladies at Independence, the forerunner of Baylor University. After eight years, they finally obtained title to
their land on the Colorado, and moved to near Marble
Falls where they lived the remainder of their lives.

While the family was living in Cat Spring, they estab-
lished a lasting friendship with the family of Johannes
Romberg, who had emigrated from Mecklenburg in
1847. Romberg was also a renowned German poet in
Texas. Eventually, two of the Fuchs sons married
Romberg daughters.

Johannes and Frederike Romberg

In the next chapter we now continue with the story as told by Caroline Mackensen Romberg.

Earliest Recollections of Our Life in Austin County

My father and mother were married in February 1856 and lived one year near Shelby, Austin County, where I was born on December 29, 1856, on my mother's birthday. When I was three weeks old, my parents moved ten miles away, to a farm my father had bought in Fayette County near Round Top, where we lived until I was four years old.

The recollections I have of my life on this place are few, because I was less than four years old when we moved again. They indicate what kinds of incidents make deep impressions on a child's mind. For instance, I remember a close neighbor, whom we called Aunt Christiane, took me home one evening. On the way we passed through a branch. I ran with all my might around a big persimmon tree for Aunt was chasing me, and I was proud that she could not catch me. I also remember visiting Aunt Louise Rotarmel one time, and I retain a picture of her pretty white house, her green lawn and a lot of red-blooming rose bushes. Another thing I remember was our well. It was under a little roof, and the water bucket was drawn by a windlass. The ground was covered with deep sand. Here Aunt Louise, who was Mother's sister, with my help filled a needle cushion that she was making for Mother. This cushion was the size of a big loaf cake. The top was covered with green checked flannel, the sides with black velvet and the bottom with black oil-cloth. Such a cushion was used when people were still sewing by hand. When a long seam was sewed, the material was pinned to this cushion; and since the cushion was very heavy, it served its purpose very well. It was in our home for many years.

I was not quite four years old when we moved to Bell County, to the place where I now live. The only remembrance I have of the trip to the new home was the crossing of a deep creek, probably the San Gabriel. It was boggy and the banks were slippery. When I followed Mother, who was leading little Anna up the slippery bank, it was still thundering; and I imagined that another large wagon was rolling up in the clouds.

When arriving in our new home in Bell County I remember how Mother and Grandmother sat down tired and discouraged, for the house had been vacant for some time and was dirty and dilapidated. Doubtless the home was soon made very cozy and liveable, for my mother was a splendid housekeeper, and father knew well how to help out by making conveniences. He had provided himself with good carpenter's tools for this pioneer life. I have the remembrance that our home was pleasant and cozy. Everything was always very clean and orderly, and our few pieces of furniture were much better than those found in the other homes around here.

Father could speak good English, but for Mother it was not so fluent. I remember seeing both seated in the winter before the fireplace, father helping Mother to learn the language. Life must have been very lonely here for Mother because the people here were strangers, and their ways and customs were different from what she was used to. Her lack of confidence in the use of the English language also made it difficult for her to associate with her new neighbors.

Seeing her homesick, father took us down to her folks for a lengthy visit. Much I remember of this visit. Unhappily an epidemic of flux spread through the country, and cousin Emmy and little Carl took it and were very ill. Then one day I saw Mother in tears. She said that little Conrad, our baby brother, had taken it too. Then Uncle Carl took sister Anna and me to good friends, where we stayed for weeks until the danger was over; but little Carl and also our little brother Conrad were taken from us. The country around Mill Creek bottoms was not so healthful as our high Bell County prairie. So our visit, so happily begun, ended sadly when we returned to Bell County.

Later, when Louis was a baby, Mother took another trip down to Austin County, this time with Mrs. Armstrong, who was visiting her people in Brenham. I think this was a very enjoyable visit for her. We girls and little Bernhard stayed at home with Father. We girls had to keep house. I was ten, sister Anna nine and Bernhard four. Of course we could not cook light bread like Mother always made, so I am sure we served cornbread. And I cannot remember what else we put on the table. Of course we had plenty of milk and butter. Churning was the most dreaded work we had, perhaps because Mother had always looked after the churning herself. Quite often after long churning the butter did not make, and washing the churn was the heaviest work we had. I sometimes doubt whether this washing was done according to the most sanitary method. Since the churn was the old style type that had a dasher, it was heavy to handle.

Sometimes Father was away from home all day, which suited us very well; for when the work was done, we could play or pass the time as we liked best. However, we were much pleased when Father told us that Mother would be back in the next few days. We tried hard to have everything neat and orderly, and we were proud when Mother praised our good housekeeping.

Pioneer Life in the Darrs Creek
Community During Civil War Times

W hen we moved to Bell County in 1860 just before the Civil War broke out, this was a beautiful rolling country covered with high grass. Here and there one could see a small bunch of cattle or horses. Along the creeks was some timber. From the hill west of our house no sign of human habitation could be seen except one corner of a fence, which enclosed a small field belonging to our nearest neighbor, Captain Dallas.

He lived with his family about one mile away down the creek towards the east and was a mighty good, kind, helpful neighbor. About two miles southeast in the prairie on a spring branch lived the Jim Armstrong family. My father always liked to go over there because they were interesting people. How unimportant was farming in those times is indicated by the following incident my father often told. He was over at the Armstrongs and mentioned something about having planted his corn. "What, is it corn planting time? Boys, where is our plow?" Evidently no one in the family had seen the plow for a long time.

A little farther south lived another neighbor, Captain Evens. His house was of brick and the best built house in this community. About two miles south of us lived Jeff Mills on the South Prong at the crossing. Then, about one mile west in the open prairie lived William Wills. This place did not have even a field. These people were cattle raisers and had only a cabin and a garden.

The only signs now left of early homesteads here are the rows of bois d'arc trees, which were at that time planted as hedges for protection of the fields against wild cattle, which had no respect for rail fences unless these were built very strong.

The houses in this vicinity were generally made of logs. They were plain, small houses, generally with a gallery in front and a lean-on in the back. The larger houses had two rooms with a hall in between and a gallery in front. This made a commodious house for that time. If these houses had more openings than a door, it would be a shutter or two for windows. These shutters did not open sideways, but upwards as in modern camp houses.

Our house consisted of three rooms. The front room was a well-built log house, well-chinked and white-washed on the inside. The other two rooms were made of rough boards perhaps sawed at the mill on the Salado River. One room was made of boards of cottonwood lumber, which looked from the distance as if it were painted white.

Our kitchen had a fireplace; but cooking was done mostly on the kitchen stove, which was the only stove in the community. There were no cupboards, only shelves to store the dishes, pots and pans. The kitchen furniture consisted of a table with a bench against the wall behind it for us children. When the shutters were open this was a right bright kitchen; but when the weather was bad and the shutters had to be kept closed, electric light would have been very pleasant.

The front room also had a large fireplace. It had two doors, one in front and one to the kitchen. In these log houses the walls could not be cut up too much, and so this room had no shutters, and the bedroom could be reached only by walking around to it on the outside.

Our front room presented an interesting picture of pioneer conditions into which an old civilization had been transplanted. The two walls adjoining the other rooms were well preserved and therefore our bookshelf and pictures were placed on these walls. The long bookshelf ran all the way across the north wall, high enough to be above the kitchen door. There were books on history, some classics and some books on agriculture. The latter were very impractical for our Texas conditions of that time. There were also books on higher mathematics, a subject in which my father was very much interested. However, in pioneer days and for many years to come he did not find time to employ himself with these books. This he did when he was an old man. He would carry a book of logarithms in his trunk when visiting his children and entertain himself with problems.

On the two protected walls were framed family pictures. I remember also an oil painting showing a village in the foreground, with the Harz mountains in the background. This was the place where my father had spent his childhood. A copy of this picture, painted by Aunt Marie Mackensen, is now in our home.

In one corner of this room was a beautiful chest of drawers with golden mahogany veneer. On it were bottles of cologne, hair pomade and sachet powder. There also was Mother's nice sewing box of mahogany veneer. The chest of drawers and the sewing box are still in our home. Both show signs of the rain that leaked down on them during the war times. Our house was covered with clapboards made of split post oak. These clapboards warped badly during heavy rains and with Father in the army there was no one to renovate the roof. I might mention here that another old piece we still have is a copper kettle, which was in pioneer days our wash kettle.

The front room was also used as bedroom, as was done in most homes in those days in this community. The bed was always placed in the corner where it was safest from rain. During heavy showers Mother placed several tin pans on the bed to catch most of the water coming down. The trundle bed underneath was a safe place for us children to hide in. I remember that we crawled in there a few times during bad rain storms and felt very safe and snug.

Perhaps the most incongruous piece in this log cabin was a large imported mirror on the south wall. It was too long for the low wall and reached up to the rafters in this room without ceiling. The mirror had a gilt frame with a decoration of golden angels at the top — among the rafters. This mirror, too, was badly damaged by rains. High up on the west wall of the room was a clock with long, heavy, hanging weights. Most of our furniture had been made by a cabinet maker in Austin County when my parents married, which was early in the year 1856.

Various things were stored on the rafters on account of shortage of room. Of these articles I shall mention only the large band box with the tall silk hat. When after the war the box was finally taken down, it was found that mice had lived in the hat and had cut a hole through the brim. In these reconstruction days when money was very scarce and things hard to get, the stovepipe came in handy as a little boy's everyday hat. The high crown was cut halfways and by folding the top over the bottom, made into a low-crowned hat that brother Bernhard, five or six years old, wore around the place for everyday.

The bed curtain, used to hide the trundle bed, also came in handy during these reconstruction days. It was made into a nice house dress for Mother, even though it was cretonne with large figures.

Our house was close to a spring, which was convenient since the water had to be carried in buckets to the house. Everybody in the community had built the house next to a spring, as springs were plentiful in this section then.

We did not have any closets like we have in these days. We had shelves and big chests in which was stored everything, Sunday shoes, hats, dress suits, linens. In the back bedroom we had three of these large chests with large locks and elaborate keys, which were all unnecessary for nothing was ever stolen. The folks of this community were plain easy-going people. Most of them were cattle raisers.

If my father had not been in the Civil War, he would doubtless have made improvements about the house, or perhaps have built a new one. The building of two new rooms was undertaken upon his return home, and the plan was to add to these later. However, we soon moved to Belton.

There were not very many slaves in this country, for there were no plantations around here, only small farms with acreage enough to raise corn and wheat for bread. No feeding of cattle, hogs or horses was done at that time. The farming utensils consisted mostly of one plow, which was drawn by one yoke of oxen.

Father moved to this place in Bell County to raise fine sheep and horses. He brought from Fayette County a large flock of sheep, of which a few merinos were imported from Germany to improve the stock. Also two shepherd dogs were imported. A large sheep barn was built—the best building on the place. My father also brought a number of fine horses and would no doubt have made a success of this undertaking if the war had not called him.

A number of those nice mares were gentle, and all had names. Mother's horse was named Fanny and was a beautiful brown pacer. Father's riding horse was named Doris and was a large bay. I was always proud when Mother came home from visiting, to sit on her nice sidesaddle and take a little ride. When I was already feeling very safe, I encouraged the horse by clucking and using the heel and stirrup. Fanny got excited, and we galloped quite a distance before I managed to pull her bridle towards home. Mother was scared and nervous, thinking that I might have an accident. I was then about six years old. It was not long before I had learned how to ride though, and I enjoyed nothing more.

The children of those pioneer days had no toys. The little girls in the vicinity played with rag dolls, and had no real dolls. The few toys sent to us by our German grandmother were very much admired by our little neighborhood friends; but these toys gradually went to pieces, and so we played with broken toys, broken dishes for instance. We had one good doll, for which we sewed dresses, aprons and bonnets

We found great pleasure in watching the lives of animals and insects — birds, snakes, lizards, frogs, wasps, bugs and ants. We were not afraid of these, for we knew their ways and knew how to distinguish the poisonous ones from the harmless ones. We really were not afraid of anything except the wild cattle. When we went to school we sometimes climbed a tree for caution until the cattle strayed to a safe distance. We learned to be careful and cautious and developed self-reliance.

During the war years my sister Anna and I had the task of watching the sheep with the youngest lambs near the farm. We were then about six or seven years old and very playful. We would forget about our duties while making play houses. When finally the mother sheep rambled on and left some of the lambs sleeping behind a bunch of grass, our trouble began. We would cautiously try to wake the lambs and get them started towards their mothers, but if one got excited and ran in a different direction, it was impossible to catch it and hard to head it off. Sometimes the only way out would be to watch it until it was tired out and lay down once more to sleep.

Then very quietly and carefully we would slip upon it and catch it to carry it back to its mother.

When we were out this way, cattle would sometimes get too close, and we would climb the trees or a fence where we felt perfectly safe until they wandered off.

One time when I was watching the lambs — I was then about ten years old — I noticed seven large longhorn steers coming across the hills in the distance. They were heading right towards me. I gathered up a lot of cow chips in my skirt, thinking that by chunking at the steers I could run them off. But when they got close, I saw that they were very fierce and so I hurried through a gap in the bois d'arc hedge which happened to be near. I expected to climb up somewhere but there was no suitable place; so I headed in full speed across the branch toward the sheep pens, these steers following me. How fast I slung through the fence I hardly remember; but not even feeling safe in the pen, I hurried up into the hayloft, where I could still hear them stamping around. Finally they disappeared, and I could go to the house. Father told us that a herd of cattle from south Texas was being driven north, that the herd had stampeded near Salado, and that these steers had evidently escaped and were on their way back to the home ranch in south Texas. These animals were large longhorn steers, much larger than our cattle in this prairie.

There were lots of wolves and coyotes in the prairie, but they were harmless. In the winter especially, they could be heard howling often night after night. The wild hogs were bad to get into the corn fields if the fences were not kept up. Down on the lower side of our field on the creek bank was a stretch of bois d'arc for fence. Where there was a skip of trees some brush was thrown in. Here the hogs had found a place to enter our corn patch at night. Mother decided that if our good shepherd dog would stay there, the hogs would keep out. So it was decided that a cot should be placed down there for us to sleep on. That would keep our dog there and protect our corn.

Father was in the army, and the corn was very necessary for food. I was not afraid to sleep there and slept fine all night. Next day the fence was repaired.

One time when breadstuff was getting scarce Mother gave Father's gold watch for four bushels of wheat. When clothing was getting scarce and nothing could be bought, Mother exchanged a beautiful shawl and some silk kerchiefs for homespun cloth, of which she made Father several good shirts which he needed very much when he came home on a furlough. I remember also that Mother tried to exchange a cutaway coat suitable for elaborate social functions, but the darkey who had something of more immediate value for Mother than this coat evidently considered the style too extreme even for war times.

Visiting in the neighborhood was done on horseback and everybody went horseback to church. The ladies were proud when they were in possession of a nice sidesaddle, a good riding skirt and a large shawl for protection instead of a coat, which was unknown at that time. People were quite sociable. To spend a day was the usual mode of visiting. Perhaps the cause of this arrangement was that neighbors lived rather far apart.

Mail was very scarce. Although we had a weekly New York paper, it was generally not brought in regularly. Neighbors would take time about bringing the mail from Salado, which was eight miles from us. One time my father had not received the paper for weeks, and so finally went to investigate. The postmaster declared the paper had not come in. Father, when looking around, saw a lot of papers under the window sill, and upon investigation, found them to be the missing papers. Perhaps the postmaster was not acquainted with our names. Mail was carried slowly over the country, and the news in the letters was not very recent.

During the warm summer days we lived more under the trees than in the house, for our house was in front of a beautiful grove of trees. Our meals were served out there for months. This life must have been a very healthful one, for we never had a doctor out during the nine years we lived there.

The Trip to Austin County

When I was seven years of age—this was during the Civil War—Mother thought it necessary for me to learn how to read. Though we had a number of books, there was nothing suitable for a beginner. An old German friend finally brought Mother a beginner's book that was an antique even at that time. The letters were very large and black; the paper rough; and the cover, instead of being made of pasteboard, was made of thin wooden boards covered with cloth. This book was entirely too difficult for beginners; the words were too long; and there were no pictures. However, I did learn to spell.

There were no schools in our neighborhood at that time; and so, when my Uncle Ohlendorf and Grandmother wrote about a good school they had at Shelby in Austin County, my mother thought it practical for me to attend that school together with my cousin Emmy, who was of my age. We found a good opportunity for me to go when Mrs. Evens, a neighbor lady, moved back to Austin County to the neighborhood of Uncle Ohlendorf.

Early one morning I was taken over to the Evens farm with all my belongings by an old hired man. There stood a large prairie schooner filled to the top with household goods. Five yoke of oxen were hitched to this heavy conveyance. In the front of the wagon was a small place for me to sit or stand in. An old darkey was the driver of this wagon. Mrs. Evens and also a black boy were on horseback. It was slow traveling. The roads were rough, and the creeks were often deep and hard to ford. The heat, the strong smell of axle grease, and perhaps the smell of parched coffee made me very ill. I often wished I could ride horseback behind Mrs. Evens. I would even have preferred to walk with the old driver, for I was strong on my feet and progress was very slow. But I did not dare mention this; besides I could not speak English very well.

We generally made a late start and did not stop at noon but stopped early in the evening for camp. I do not remember getting anything to eat or drink during the day. Camp was generally near a farm house. I certainly was glad to get out of the high wagon back to the ground. A chair was always taken down for Mrs. Evens to sit on while the darkeys unhitched the oxen and cooked supper at a big fire. Sometimes the ladies of the farm would visit for a while with Mrs. Evens. Perhaps they were old acquaintances of Mrs. Evens, for the few scattered settlers along the road were known far and wide.

One night when camping in this way, a lady with two little children came to visit. After playing for some time, the children asked me to go to the house with them, which was nearby, and play hide and seek in the moonlight. I was not much impressed with that game as I was not acquainted with the place. It was too dark around the house, so I decided to go back to the camp. After climbing the rail fence which enclosed the yard, I lost sight of the camp fire down the road. Being sure of the direction, I started straight on, but got into the woods. When I realized that I was lost, I called for Mrs. Evens. In a few minutes a Negro woman was there to carry me back to the camp, which was only a little distance away. I was so upset that I even cried. Mrs. Evens in her kindness gave me a cup of right black coffee to drink, which was the only delicacy at her disposal. Although it was bitter as gall, I drank a little to please her and then went to bed on the pallet which had been prepared for me.

There were no bridges at that time, and some fords were very steep and sometimes boggy. When crossing the Brushy Creek, which was exceptionally deep, the wagon wheels were locked with chains. The first pair of the five yokes of oxen was already down by the water when I, in the wagon, was still up on the high bank. I was in great fear that the wagon would turn over. The old darkey, however, knew his business. The locked wheels made the wagon go down like a slide, and we got down safely. To this day I remember how, with both the men busy cracking their long whips and encouraging the oxen with a lot of shouting, we pulled up the steep bank.

After five days of this traveling, we arrived at the home of Mrs. Evens' daughter. After a few days Uncle Carl Ohlendorf arrived to take me home with him. How happy I was when after this long trip with strangers, I saw his kind, familiar face. I rode back of him on his big horse.

One time we stopped; and he got down to light his pipe, which was not as easy as it is in these days. First he filled his pipe with tobacco, then got out the tinder box, flintrock and steel; the first two he placed close together in his hands, striking the flint with the steel. This caused sparks which lit the tinder. Then the tinder box was held upside down on the tobacco. This was the way all people lit their pipes, for no one had matches during the Civil War.

When arriving at Uncle's house, I noticed with great pleasure the pretty yard fence, the roomy house with glass windows. Grandmother and Aunt rushed out to meet me with many endearments while the children looked on with astonishment. All this and the hearing of the familiar language caused me to thaw out again.

Next day, on Monday, I started to school with cousin Emmy. The schoolhouse was a good frame building with plenty of glass windows, inside sheeting, long good benches with inkstands screwed in along the top, and a good desk for the teacher, but no recitation bench. While we read aloud and recited, we stood up at our seats and then sat down again. One book, a slate and pencil were our equipment. The slate was very essential. The teacher was very strict with his students of whom there were about fifty. No whispering was allowed. Punishments were a daily occurrence. The only time I was really homesick was when I was punished for speaking out loud to cousin Emmy while the teacher had left the room and had put in charge some student who stood there with a slate in his hand. Of course I did not understand that it was against the rule to speak. When recess came, I was told to stay in for punishment while all the rest ran out to play. When I broke out crying, the girls crowded around me in sympathy. I struck at them with my hands and wished I could be back at home. This was, however, the only time I had to stay in.

Later I enjoyed my school life and my life down there with my relatives. I stayed nearly two years. The community life there was much more interesting, more stimulating and enjoyable than in Bell County. The colony was older and had already made more progress in social life.

One should not criticize too strictly the teacher's methods; for with fifty scholars of all grades, he must have kept very busy. Besides, there were few books to aid in the instruction, no arithmetic, no geographies, only a reader which contained also a little grammar. All arithmetic problems the teacher wrote down on the slates, then later he checked them over. Writing was very essential; and much time was given to written exercises, which were mostly done on a slate and, after being corrected by the teacher, were copied with ink on paper. We did not always have steel pens, and I remember writing at times with a goose quill, which Uncle knew how to cut with a pen knife. This pen made heavy lines; and since our paper was very thin and the ink showed through, our exercises presented a very muddled appearance. Father and Mother were highly pleased with the progress I had made in this school in the less than two years.

My trip back to Bell County was easier than the trip down. A minister's family visited down there, and they were kind enough to bring me back home. They traveled in a hack drawn by horses. At night they stopped over with friends. Generally a small community religious meeting was held at such a home at night by Brother Houchins.

One of the stops was at the home of Captain Dallas, our neighbor; and the grown daughters of the house were delighted to take me home. While still a good distance from our house, they already started out calling "Caroline has come." Sister and baby Bernhard had grown to my surprise; and even my little brother Louis met me toddling on his little bow legs. Father and Mother had not changed much and were of course very glad to have me back, for I was always the lively one in the family.

Changes After the Civil War

With the close of the Civil War, a lot of changes took place. School was opened up in our neighborhood. Even though I was a child, I was astonished at the difference in the way in which school was conducted here and in Austin County. At that time only private schools existed. Teachers were scarce and anyone willing could teach. The school here usually closed after a few months, the teacher finding some more profitable occupation.

After the Civil War a number of new settlers came to this community. First young men came from the war and from the older states to get a new start in this open country. Also numerous families came from the other Confederate states. The old settlers here at that time enlarged their farms to rent out to these newcomers, and a farming community soon developed.

After the war, too, a number of the roaming cattle were gathered and driven to Kansas. Our neighbor, Captain Dallas, drove a large herd he had collected here and in Burnet County to Kansas, where he sold it. But he had the misfortune to be swindled out of the payment, for he was given a false draft.

Several weddings occurred during this time in our neighborhood. First Miss Marion Mills, who lived two miles south on the Darrs Creek, had a big wedding supper served under an arbor with dancing later. There I heard my first instrumental music in this community; which, I suppose, consisted of one or two fiddles. People were anxious for a little social activity after the depressing war years. I had the opportunity of attending this wedding as Miss Lizzie Dallas offered to take me along. Captain Dallas was a very pious church member and allowed no dances and no attendance at dances; but as he was absent on the trip to Kansas, and his daughters were anxious to attend the wedding, they obtained permission from the kind stepmother to do so. Soon after, Miss Mary Dallas married Mr. Stafford, who came from Tennessee. This wedding was also a big social event which we attended. Here also a big supper was served — with eggnog. While there, we had a heavy rain and coming home was no picnic. Mother with baby and me — behind — were on horseback. Since it was pitch dark Papa led the horse. When coming to our creek bank, which was steep and slippery, I had to dismount and walk. Since it was so dark, I had some trouble to follow up. I crossed the creek with my Sunday shoes on. I waited for the lightning before attempting to ascend the bank on which I even slipped. Then I watched carefully for the lightning to locate the horse and Father and Mother. To my horror I often was far behind. And under the trees, where it was especially dark, I ran against a tree but finally got to the house safely.

It was easy for young people to marry, as very little was needed for housekeeping. The children of Captain Dallas all received 160 acres of land with some cattle and horses, so that they had some property; but their home and their mode of living was very simple. The young husband erected a plain house mostly of logs. It had the necessary fireplace, of course. Very little furniture was necessary, just a bed, a few chairs and a table on which to eat. The kitchen utensils consisted of a few pots and pans. The coffee pot must not be forgotten, for everybody drank coffee in those days. The very few dishes were generally stored on a shelf, for there were no cupboards and closets. Of course husband and wife both owned a nice saddle and a riding horse; for these afforded the only method of traveling either to the neighbors, the church, or the nearest town, where now, after the war, the stores were once more offering goods for sale.

Looms and spinning wheels were discarded after the war. Of course, money was scarce and goods were high; so there was a limit to buying. People still dressed plainly and were contented with their simple mode of life. No doubt the women were glad that spinning and carding had had their day; for while it was no hard work to do this, it took up so much time.

The homespun goods had to be dyed, which was quite an art and looked very interesting to me. One time a neighbor lady with her son rode up to do some dyeing in mother's large copper kettle. They had sacks of leaves, roots, barks and berries. Perhaps they also had some chemicals which helped to make different dyes. The most interesting part of the process was taking out of the dye the big hanks of yarn in different pretty colors.

During the war I enjoyed seeing the spinning, and I would have loved trying the loom. All of this work seemed so easy to do. Mother had only a small spinning wheel on which only wool could be spun. Out of this wool were made socks and stockings for winter, which people had to make at home or do without. Spinning on the little wheel was restful work; but when spinning with a large wheel—large as wagon wheel—one had to walk incessantly backwards and forwards.

A good many changes took place after the close of the war; but the dilapidated building used as both church and schoolhouse was not improved. Although there were a number of children, no good teacher could be secured. I had probably made very little progress since I had left Mr. Eversberg's school in Austin County. In order to give us better schooling, our parents decided to move to Belton.

When I returned from Austin County, I had to read to Mother every day, and I had to teach sister Anna to read. Another duty was to learn how to knit and sew. As there were no sewing machines at that time, every girl had to know how to sew by hand. We had to sew our under-clothes, making neat seams and using the different stitches. This had to be done very neatly or it had to be taken out and done over again. We must have been able to sew very well, for we spent much time sewing doll clothes. I have always been thankful for Mother's good instruction, for I have had much sewing to do in my life; and even now in my old age, I still enjoy sewing.

School in the Darrs Creek Community

The opening of school in Holland naturally brings to my mind the school of this community as it was some seventy years ago. Of course, there was no Holland then. The country was sparsely settled. My parents, in 1860, moved from Austin County to Bell County, to the place where I now live. At that time I could see from the hill west of our house no sign of human habitation, outside of our own homestead, except a corner of the fence that enclosed the small field on Captain Dallas' place, which was about a mile west of where Holland now is.

The school house of the community was located about half a mile west of the present Holland on the north side of the Darrs Creek, where a spring furnished good water. The one-room box house had no windows but wooden shutters, which could be opened to let in the light. The room could be heated by a fireplace; however, the top part of the chimney had fallen down and so no large fires could be built. Consequently, on real cold days school was not kept. The benches were split logs smoothed a bit on top. These primitive benches were placed around the walls of the room so that the pupils could rest their backs against the wall. There was no blackboard, no teacher's seat. However, there was a recitation bench and a small desk in one corner of the room where one could do some writing—if one felt so inclined. I remember that I sat there sometimes—mainly to show off my writing ability. I had received good training in an Austin County school. No trees surrounded the school house, so the cattle would collect on the shady side of the building. During a rainy spell they would mire up the place considerably.

School would get started somewhat in this manner: A person desiring to teach would arrive in the community and express his wishes to some prominent citizen, perhaps Captain Dallas, who would then send someone around to the neighbors; and if enough pupils could be rounded up for a term of a few months, school would be opened. Pupils included grown young men and young ladies as well as children. When finally so many dropped out of school that it was not a paying proposition any more, the teacher would move on to another community. One time our teacher and his family lived in a tent during their sojourn.

Books were scarce, so the course of study was very simple. Every pupil brought the books he had and learned out of that supply. Families that had more school books than they needed were accommodating and lent to others less fortunate. Some children had only a speller — the famous "blue backed" speller. The McGuffey readers were also important text books. If a child had finished the first reader, and a second was not to be had, he would start with the third reader next. A slate was used for writing and arithmetic — if one had a slate. I should mention that one boy had a grammar and studied it.

The methods of teaching were simple. First the beginner learned the alphabet, then he learned to spell, and finally he somehow miraculously learned to read. There were some who in later years could still rattle off by memory the entire first column of words in the "blue backed" speller because so much time and effort had been spent on the difficult beginning. In the back of the speller was a list of long words; individuality, indivisibility, incomprehensibility, and so on. Everybody knew where that list was, and it was everybody's ambition to spell out that list some day to perfection and with great speed with the entire school as an admiring audience.

Imagine a little girl holding a speller in her hand all day long with no desk to lay it on. To prevent the book from wearing out where the thumb pressed down and formed a sweaty, dirty place, a device was used that is unknown to the present generation of students. This device was a "thumb paper." One placed a small piece of paper on the proper spot of the page, and then put the thumb on the paper. That "thumb paper" was very important. In time it became more and more elaborate and decorative. Some children cut out a little heart, others used a piece of colored paper — not often seen in those days — or they used strips of colored papers braided together. The "thumb paper" certainly added interest to an otherwise dry page.

The teacher probably realized the tedium of learning out of a speller and similarly difficult books and overlooked conversation when the speller was held up as a screen. It was also permissible to go to the spring on the pretext of getting a drink. There one could play in the water a while and eat a snack that had been smuggled out of the school room. If one forgot the time and stayed too long, one might be asked to stand in the middle of the school room as punishment for the transgression.

The chief diversion of the noon-day recess was wading in the creek, hunting grapes and nuts and making chewing gum from the inner bark of the gum-elastic tree. One pealed off the outer rough bark to procure the inner bark. This was then chewed vigorously, though it was very bitter; and then the entire mass was balled together and rubbed and pulled in running water, usually by one of the larger girls, so that the particles of wood washed out. It was fine art to chew the bark to just the right consistency; for if it was chewed too much, small pulp would not wash out; and if it was not chewed enough, too much of the valuable gum was lost. Finally the finished delicacy was divided among the group. The stuff was very stretchy and was excellent material for blowing bubbles. It sometimes happened that the teacher got tired of the whole mess and the disturbance created thereby, and forbade further chewing. It also happened that a good friend would ask, "Let me chew your gum a while." Ideas about sanitation were very vague.

Most of the pupils rode to school on horseback. Since the teacher had no watch or clock, punctuality was unimportant. It was customary to bring a jar or bottle of milk far lunch. The first comers set their jars in the spring, later ones stuck theirs in the mud around the spring to keep the milk cool. All this could be turned into an awful mess if stray pigs came along while the pupils were in the school room.

One time a teacher opened a writing school which the young ladies and young men of the neighborhood attended.an hour or two each day for a few weeks. Another time we had a two-teacher school. The wife of the teacher taught the beginners to spell. During the recitation she would occasionally ask her husband, "Mr. Wilson, how do you pronounce this word?"

My parents finally moved to Belton in order to secure better schooling for their children than was possible in the Darrs Creek community right after the Civil War. Other families moved to or sent their children to Salado, which was then already well known for its excellent college.

We Move to Belton and Have New
Experiences and Impressions

I t was May, 1870—I was then thirteen years old—
when we moved to Belton, where Father had
bought a place. We children of course expected
much of this change. We loved the old farm and hoped
to be back quite often—but did not go back for years.

The last thing we saw as we drove off was brother
Bernhard's collection of white skulls, which were
grouped under a small grove of trees outside the yard.
He was very proud of his collection and would have
liked to take it along, which was, of course, impossible.
The rest of us children helped him collect his specimens.
Whenever we found an odd-looking skull, we brought it
home to him. Father declared that some day Bernhard
would be a naturalist, which eventually turned out to be
a correct prediction. In his collection he had heads of cattle, buffaloes, horses, sheep, dogs, skunks, opossums,
wolves, snakes, and so on. He even had different sizes of
each kind. Whenever we did not know to what animal
the head could have belonged, we consulted Father. This
enthusiasm for collecting indicates that even though our
contacts with other people were few, we had many interests to fill out our days.

The Belton home was better than our old home, but
still there was lots of work. The house had not been occupied for some time, so we girls had to help to get everything in order. We did not have time to be homesick
for our old home and friends.

We three oldest children were soon started in a small
private school conducted by a lady, Miss Belle Shelton.
This preliminary schooling was very beneficial for us,

for it prepared us for entrance into the big school that opened in September.

After everything was in smooth running order on the new place in Belton, Father looked after his interests on the farm where he built several rent houses, fenced in all the land and put it in cultivation. Because he made these improvements on the land, which I think was half a section, he was absent from home a good deal.

After a union Sunday school was organized by Mr. and Mrs. McWhirter, Mother saw to it that we attended; for we had not had an opportunity to attend Sunday school before.

At this time, in the early seventies, the large cattle drives to Kansas started. They passed right by our house, which was on the edge of town. Of course these drives were interesting to us children who had grown up on the prairies and had seen cattle all of our lives. One rider headed the herd and was generally followed by a few large longhorn steers, which were the leaders. These herds extended over a mile, so it seems to me now, and moved forward in a cloud of dust. It was pitiful to see the last stragglers that could hardly keep up, generally cows and calves.

Another interesting event was the coming of the circus every fall of the year. In those days the wagons and cages moved through the country drawn by horses. The tents were always erected between our house and town. With fascination we watched tree interesting work of erecting the tents and the other preparations. Customary at that time was the parade with its loud band, which was enjoyed by people from all over the country.

Another new experience for us in Belton was attending the large school when it opened in the fall. This school, like all schools of this time, was a private institution. Some years later, when my father attended a meeting in the interest of establishing a public school, a prominent citizen made the following remark: "We don't want a public school. It is not democratic."

Our school building contained only one large room divided by a partition about five feet high on one side of which sat the girls and on the other side the boys. A platform extended all the way across one side of the building. On this platform sat the teachers, and on this platform were held the recitations, several of which went on at the same time.

One feature of the instruction I liked especially was singing. Mrs. Moore, one of the teachers had a melodium which she had brought to school and on which she accompanied the songs. I was anxious to take music lessons; but Father thought that the lessons were too expensive; and furthermore, he did not have much faith in the teaching ability of the ladies that gave instruction. The first musical instrument we had was a music box which could play two pieces. Its tones were very clear and beautiful. The next instrument was a large harmonica on which we could soon play anything we wanted to. Sooner than expected, my parents gave me the opportunity to take the piano lessons I so earnestly desired.

Two Years of Instruction in Burnet County

One summer when Father had made a business trip to his friend, Edward Ebeling, a well-to-do ranchman in Burnet County, he returned with the news that Mr. Ebeling had employed a tutor for his children who was quite a musician, that a new piano was in the house, and that children were instructed in music. Mother and Father decided that here was a good opportunity for us to learn music and at the same tire to continue my German along with English and other studies. So my clothes were put in readiness, and then Father and I started in a wagon on the trip to Burnet County. I was then fifteen years old.

We traveled all day on a rough road, passing only a few houses of scattered settlers. It was a tiresome and hot drive. The water keg was new, which made the water taste strongly of pine. Being warm, it tasted like medicine to me. I was nauseated and felt very miserable. I wanted nothing more than good sour milk. Father was dubious about finding any in this desolate country with its few settlers living in small cabins. However when we finally came by a small farm, Father tried to find milk. The woman living there had just finished churning and Father brought me nearly a gallon bucket of fresh buttermilk. This refreshing milk revived me, and next morning I felt much better and was glad to resume the trip. We stopped this first night at Brooksfield, near Florence.

The second day we came through country that was still more rough and still less settled. That night we stopped with friends and were well taken care of. These folks related several incidents of recent horse stealing and robberies. Some people thought that these depreda-

tions were done by Indians, but Father did not agree
with this explanation. Next day we got into the heavy
cedar brakes with awful rocky roads. Looking at the
dense growth on both sides of the road, I thought of the
accounts I had heard the night before, and got nervous.
Besides, Father had a loaded pistol within easy reach,
which was very unusual for him. I suppose he must
have considered the pistol necessary for protection. Of
course, I never mentioned my fear to Father, but I kept a
close outlook to the right and left. Finally we reached the
Colorado River where the country was more settled, and
my fears were abated.

We arrived at Mr. Ebeling's on a Sunday afternoon.
There were visitors at the house, and I met three girls,
sisters, about my age, who were to be my good friends
later. Their parents, Mr. and Mrs. von Varnhagen, were
visiting a relative of Professor Heinrich Fuchs, who was
to be my teacher.

Professor Fuchs was an elderly gentleman, with long
white beard and long white hair. He was a scholar and a
fine musician. There were hardly any schools in this
thinly settled country, and the well-to-do ranchmen employed a private teacher as Mr. Ebeling did for his two
boys, Otto and Rudolph of twelve and fourteen. I
proudly showed the professor the books that I had used
in Belton, but he discarded them and taught mainly
without books. We studied English, German and Span-
ish, music and other customary subjects under him. We
had to do a great deal of writing. The grammar was
taught incidentally. In the morning we studied in the
school room; in the afternoon we had mainly music and
writing; and at night we had to read aloud to the professor out of good books from his excellent private library.
He was a good teacher in academic subjects; but although he was an excellent musician, he lacked ability to
teach beginners.

He was an especial admirer of Wagner's music, which was new at that time. I remember that he complained to Mr. Ebeling that the piano should have seven octaves instead of only six and three fourths octaves. Thereupon Mr. Ebeling stated that the piano could be sold to a neighbor and a new piano bought. This pleased the old professor very much. The piano was to stay at the Ebeling home until the new piano arrived; but Miss Doolittle, the private teacher at the nearby Burnham ranch, was to come over with her three charges and teach them at the Ebeling home. I always stayed in the room while she gave her piano lessons and profited a great deal. Although the old professor did not think so highly of her musicianship, she was a very capable teacher for beginners.

The old professor was very solicitous that I should have social contacts; and he saw to it that I visited with his relatives, who were well educated and refined people. I enjoyed these contacts very much, especially in the Varnhagen home, where the professor had formerly been a tutor and where he still visited frequently.

The old professor was a dear old gentleman, and I thought a great deal of him. I was very much grieved when he was drowned in attempting to cross a rising stream that was much more dangerous than it had appeared to be. The new instructor was also an old scholarly gentleman. Our music lessons were continued under Miss Doolittle.

I profited greatly by the two years in the Ebeling home because of the excellent instruction under private teachers and also because of the environment. Mr. Ebeling and my father were very good friends who had already known each other in their youth. Mr. Ebeling was therefore like a father to me. His sister, Miss Ebeling, who looked after us, was a dear old soul; and the boys were like brothers. Other friends I have not mentioned were the [Rudolph] Richters, who were also very good friends of my father. A granddaughter in this house, Meta Stuckert, later Mrs. Heinrich Ulrich, was one of my very best friends.

During the second summer, Father and sister Anna came for me, and I returned home. I was then seventeen.

When I Was a Young Lady

As I was beginning to have the interests of a young lady, I was very much pleased with our new house, which had been built during my absence. It had five rooms, a hall and a nice porch; and it was painted gray with white trimmings.

Life was almost too easy with no lessons and with no piano to practice on. We attended Sunday school and church, went to parties and picnics and visited quite a bit. Sister Anna and I helped to keep the house neat; we sewed and made fancy work, such as hand-made laces and embroidery. Such ornamental work was very fashionable then and took much time.

We were very anxious for the new piano to come, but some time passed before the instrument arrived from Boston. It was the first upright piano in Belton, most of the pianos of that time being square. Of course we were highly pleased with the beauty of the instrument and the beauty of its tone. I had not played since I left the Ebelings. When Mother said, "Now play us a piece," I probably also had a little stage fright for all stood around and looked on, and so the performance was not so successful. However, I soon improved; for I spent much time practicing. I also gave piano lessons to sister Anna and the boys.

Some of my time was taken up with reading articles and continued stories in the *New Yorker Wochenblatt*, which was an excellent weekly paper, then widely read, and which had been in our home as long as I could remember.

Sister Anna and I were of the age when dressing is of great importance, and so we spent much time sewing and keeping ourselves provided with attractive clothes. As commercial patterns were unheard of, we like others used patterns that were passed from friend to friend. Perhaps the original was once cut by a seamstress, or it may have been homemade. Anyway, we spent much time trying on and resewing seams of the tightfitting basks that had so many seams and stays to make them fit correctly. The overskirt and the crazy style of the bustle were then in vogue. Skirts were down to the floor, and plenty of petticoats were worn. Waists were as small as possible.

So far sister Anna and I had not been back to the old farm and the Darrs Creek community; but we kept up with our friends pretty well, because they came to Belton to make their purchases and to visit us. Sometimes they came to dinner and at other tines they spent the night. Belton had a number of good stores and was the county seat, so people from far and wide came to Belton. Temple was unheard-of, and the railroads had not been built.

Finally in 1876 Father took us for a four days visit to our old friends. A camp meeting was in progress, and we had the opportunity of seeing everybody. We found the community had changed much. Only towards Salado there was still some open prairie. In all other directions from our old home we saw farms and new farm houses. Our old friends had moved into comfortable homes and everything looked prosperous.

Before we had moved to Belton, the place where Holland is now had one little store with a post office called Mountain Home. Later when the railroad was built through in about 1880, the place was named Holland, probably after Colonel Holland, a prominent citizen.

The camp meeting which we attended was held in a grove of large trees, where a commodious arbor had been erected. The location was on the Darrs Creek east of the present highway bridge. The people gathered about ten in the morning with their baskets of food for dinner and supper. At night we went home with our friends; and so we visited the Armstrongs, the Shaws, Goodes and Dallas. We had a grand time, but I must admit that we were pretty tired when we got home. We had missed lots of sleep, for wherever we spent the night we talked late. And the farm women got up early to fix breakfast and to prepare another luncheon basked in which fried chicken, biscuits and pies took a prominent place.

In 1876 Father bought Mr. Denny's general merchandise business. Mr. Ben Decherd, who had been with this store for years was taken in as partner. The business house was located on the north side of the square, where the main business houses were located. That my father had won friendship and respect in Belton is evident from the fact that he was elected as mayor a few years later.

Mother liked this home in town very much. Everything was so much more convenient, and there was more company. There was more to see and to hear. She was fond of company, but never visited much. As a hostess, she could never do enough for her guests. She was small, slender, graceful and always held herself straight. She had a heavy suit of brown hair, which she always kept as neat as her dresses were. I always associate with her picture a neat white collar.

Sister Anna and I were very different. She was slim, delicate, timid; while I was lively and quick and had more weight.

Father did not permit our boys to hang around town. Whenever they were not in school, they had work to do at home, such as taking care of the chickens, cows and the team. Whenever the boys wanted to use Father's excellent carpenter tools they could so, provided they took care of these tools. One time they built in the yard a little house that was in all details just like a real house.

Passers-by stopped to admire it. Another time they
made a little wagon with a frame, to which the calves
were hitched. The calves were so tame that they could
very well represent the ox teams that were still seen on
the roads at that time. Of course the boys liked to go
hunting to chase rabbits with their dogs. When their
beloved dog Ranger died, the boys buried him and provided a tombstone with an epitaph. Later Bernhard
wrote "The Story of the Life of Ranger." Rereading this
story in later years, he was amused how often he came
across the phrase "and a fierce struggle ensued." Probably he adopted this and other similar expressions from
the histories which he liked to read. He was an avid
reader and borrowed books from friends to supplement
the generous supply we already had at home. When the
Agricultural and Mechanical College was opened, every
county could send two students free. Brother Bernhard
won this appointment.

Louis was a very industrious little fellow. Unlike
Bernhard, he had lots of temper and would get into
fights with other boys. Such differences were then
smoothed over for him by the easy-going Bernhard.
Each boy had a calf, which was taken care of and later
sold. Louis always had better luck with his calves and
sold them for better price. He was very conscientious
about taking care of the animals on the place, and he enjoyed planting things. Later when he was at college, his
subject was agronomy.

There was never any fussing or dissension in our
family. Ours was a peaceful home. Father and Mother
were very neat and orderly, and we children were
trained in the sane way. My father was naturally a leader
in his community. He had very excellent judgment and a
good education; he was honest, fair and just. For him
there was no compromise between right and wrong. Besides he had traveled more, seen more countries and met

more types of people than most of his associates had. He had a good memory and was an animated and interesting conversationalist. He was my ideal of what a man should be — however I was soon to meet a younger version of my ideal.

Engagement and Wedding

Through correspondence I had kept up with my friends in Burnet County. In August, 1878, when my father again had to make a business trip to the Ebeling ranch and I was invited for a visit, I was delighted to go. Traveling was not as strenuous as before, as the country was more settled and the roads better; consequently, it took less time to make the trip.

We first stopped with our friends, the Richters, for a visit. My friend Meta was at home, and her sister Hermine was also home from Austin for a visit. These girls told me all the news about their amusements, picnics, little dances at private homes, and about the new persons who had come into the neighborhood. Most of these new comers were young men interested in the now flourishing sheep business. They were well educated and of good families and added much interest to the local gatherings.

Very often they mentioned a Mr. Romberg, who was now tutoring the Ebeling boys. He had studied in Europe, traveled in the north, had come to visit his married sisters—who lived in the neighborhood—and had temporarily accepted the position of tutor at the Ebelings. With so much admiration for this gentleman, my curiosity was properly stimulated to meet him at this ranch, where we were expected to visit. On the coming Sunday afternoon, a very hot one, Father took Meta and me over there. As we alighted, everyone rushed out to greet us, including Mr. Romberg. It was the first time I shook hands with this important person. After a week's visit Father decided to go back to Bell County to bring up some loads of flour milled from the wheat grown on our farm. I was to remain till he returned. Could the two old friends have wanted to give Amor an opportunity? No need to mention that the visit was a very enjoyable one for me. My girl friends stayed with me for several weeks; we played games — croquet, for instance — went visiting together, danced.

Mr. Ebeling suggested one evening that with young ladies in the house, evidently good dancers who would enjoy a little dancing, there was a good opportunity for his bashful boys to improve their steps. I made the remark that I was afraid that I would not be of much help as in Belton we had danced mostly square dances. Mr. Romberg then suggested that it would be a good time to improve my dancing too — and he seemed right glad to do his part.

Mr. Romberg was a tall and slim and very agile person. He was a good conversationalist, ready to tease, quick in repartee. The time for instruction was in the afternoon. When he and his two students were on the back gallery — a cool, quiet and secluded place — we could hear him lecture at times. He had a method of walking up and down while lecturing. Since he could play both the piano and the violin, he also gave music lessons to the boys.

To make a long story short, we fell in love and were engaged — secretly, we thought. The courtship had had its difficulties, for there was no privacy anywhere. In that community, young folks just did not go walking, so this Mr. Romberg offered to teach me checkers. Under cover of this absorbing game, a few words could sometime be exchanged in private.

Since my father's return had been delayed beyond his expectations, there was time for me to visit the sisters of my fiancé, who were Louise Fuchs and Caroline Fuchs. It was November before we started home — this time over Austin. On the morning of our start home, the weather was very cloudy and sultry; and after we had crossed the Pedernales and were on the high Shingle

Knob mountain, a severe norther with snow overtook us. On the trip up to Burnet County Father had noticed a new school building in this neighborhood where he hoped we could stay over night. We arrived there about four o'clock. The children were waiting for their father to take them home. In the school house was a large fireplace with glowing logs. The people who came for the children were very friendly, and told us to stay there and keep a good fire burning. Mother had seen to it that we had good bedding for the return trip, so we slept very well before the fire. Travel next day was slow and cold. For the night we had to camp in the woods. Father and Sil Cline, the tenant from our farm, who was driving an extra wagon, made a fire by a fallen tree. I slept very soundly in the wagon which was put on the south side of the fire while Father and Mr. Cline slept on the ground. They had placed their bedding on a rawhide to keep it dry. Father and Mr. Cline attended to the preparation of the food. Everything in Austin was covered with snow and ice. The place looked cold and quiet, so we drove through without stopping. However the weather moderated, and we got home on the fourth day without any mishaps.

Our wedding was originally planned for the following September. My fiancée had accepted the Cypress Mill school and lived with his sister Louise. However in spring, during the lambing season, there was a vacation of several weeks as the boys had to help with the flocks. So he suggested that we have our wedding during this vacation because there was a nice vacant house conveniently near his sister's home. Besides, we could use his sister's hack for a honeymoon trip to his folks. Then, in the lively family of his sister, he had no place for concentration and study. There were other very good reasons. So I agreed and set the third Thursday in March as the wedding day. Later I found that this would be on the fifteenth, which gave me very little time to get ready.

We got very busy at home to prepare for the wedding. Mother was anxious to supply her oldest daughter well for the new home; and for that day and time, I was indeed amply supplied. Besides the usual sheets, pillow cases and silver, I had bedding, kitchenware, irons, a lamp, churn and many other things. Many of these articles my father had in his store.

Our wedding was to be a small home wedding. Our very good friend, Mrs. Ulrich, and her daughter helped us to get everything ready. We were to serve cake and wine, fruits and nuts — all of which was just to be passed around.

At that time a wedding was not announced ahead of time as it is now; the parties concerned tried to have it a great surprise. I intended to conform to this custom, so I instructed Father earnestly not to mention anything to his friends. He thought this was very foolish, but to please me he promised to say nothing. The day before the wedding suspicions were aroused for then the groom arrived and went to town with Father to buy a wedding suit. This suit was of black broadcloth. The frock coat — which we still have upstairs in the big chest — with its skirts reaching nearly to the knees, was fashionable then for state occasions. A white vest was worn with this coat.

I invited the guests myself on the morning of the wedding day [March 15, 1877]. It was not customary then for all friends and acquaintances to make elaborate presents. My wedding dress was of white linen lawn with embroidery. It had been cut to fit — so we thought — by a dressmaker and finished by me. Since there was so much to do, I never once took time to try it on. I was terribly upset when this princess dress with its long row of pearl buttons in the back was too tight fitting to close. Of course the wedding had to come off, and the dress had to be worn. So we cut off the buttons, took out the hem, tacked the buttons on to the button holes, and closed the dress with pins. At the appointed time the marriage was solemnized. We had an Episcopal minister, and used the ring ceremony. I was glad when the ceremony was over. Later the Belton band, which Will Douthitt conducted, serenaded us. This broke the spell of solemnity. We asked the musicians in for refreshments and ended the evening with a little dancing.

On the honeymoon trip we first visited my kinfolks, the Ohlendorfs, who still lived in their former home at Shelby. Grandmother had the same custom of sitting by her window — in the same chair as formerly; but it was not necessary for her to knit and spin now, as formerly, for socks and knitted jackets could be bought everywhere. Cousin Emmy was married, too, and lived with her husband, Herman von Roeder, in Industry, where he was teaching. The two young husbands, who had met for the first time, found many common interests. Cousin Emmy and I talked much about the past and future. We had much in common and looked at life much in the same way. This has been more evident as the years have passed.

Next we went to Fayette County and stopped first with Aunt Frederike Perlitz. It happened that her five little girls were visiting with Grandfather and Grandmother Romberg, so Aunt Frederike decided that she also would go to the parents and introduce me as her neighbor, Mrs. Lewis. The masquerade was not very successful. When Grandmother and Aunt Ida came out, they recognized me at once; the young husband came out of his hiding and joined the group; and the rejoicing was great.

Then started a week of visiting with sisters and brothers, cousins, aunts and uncles, the old teacher Sturke in

High Hill, the good friend and companion on the European trip — Werner Perlitz — now also married and living in Schulenburg. At the last place we had for dinner peaches that had been canned in a glass jar. It was my first acquaintance with a fruit jar. The filled jar was passed around and everybody examined it with interest.

I liked the Romberg family, but since they were all elderly people — except the Frankes — I felt very young and inexperienced. It was difficult for me at first to call the dignified people by their first names and to use the familiar address. They were people of culture, very unpretentious, cordial and sincere. I realized that I had married into a family that I could love and respect.

Our Home at Cypress Mill

From now on, in this account, I shall drop the use of such expressions as "Mr. Romberg" or "the young husband" and instead, since this is written primarily for my children, I shall say "your father" or simply "Father." There cannot be confusion when referring to my own father, for from now on my life was not as constantly and intimately connected with my father's as it was when I was at home and under his personal protection and guidance.

On the trip from Fayette County to Cypress Mill we stopped at Austin to buy some furniture and have our pictures taken. My parents had given me a check to buy a table and chairs and a solid walnut bedroom suit, the dresser and small washstand of which are still in our home. Grandmother had given me ten dollars to buy a clock, the one my son Louis has now. My generous parents had provided me with so many things that the only necessities we had to buy in order to start housekeeping were a cook stove, some dishes and groceries. These purchases and also the other things shipped from Belton to Austin were hauled to Cypress Mill by Uncle Wilhelm Fuchs' teamster by ox team. Oxen were used at that time because they could stand the rough road better than horses, and they could pull better through the almost impassable Pedernales crossing.

When our things arrived it was a great pleasure to arrange everything in our new home. We were very proud of our possessions, for we were better fitted than most young couples in the vicinity.

In this first house, which was within calling distance of Aunt Louse, we lived only a few months. Your father was much in favor of buying a small ranch that was for sale. The residence of this ranch was only about two miles away from Cypress Mill. As we bought this ranch from a Mr. Cleveland, we always spoke of it as our Cleveland place. We bought with the condition that the Clevelands were to keep the residence until next spring. However, your father was so anxious to move out there and to take charge that we walked over one day to inspect the old rent houses of which only one was empty. It had not been lived in for a long time and was certainly ugly and dilapidated. The inside was very black but the roof and floor were good. We made it liveable with repairs, plenty of whitewash, and a new canvas for ceiling; and then we moved in. Here our first little boy arrived [March 30, 1878]. We named him after both grandfathers Otto John Romberg. When he was three weeks old, we moved into the Cleveland residence, a roomy, comfortable, old-style house. We lived on the Cleveland place five years and enjoyed it, for it was a nice place in a good community.

Cypress Mill was a sort of village with a saw mill, grist mill, store, post office, blacksmith shop, and wheelwright shop. Several families lived either in the village or nearby.

One of the most influential persons here was Aunt Louise Fuchs, who presided over a large household. Besides taking care of her own large family, she boarded usually several hired men and several young men who were maybe friends of the family and were perhaps establishing themselves in the sheep or cattle business. She was a very healthy woman, a very capable and efficient manager. Her good husband helped her in many ways. I am surprised how she found so much time to visit. Of course it was not necessary at that time to spend much time on fine clothes, though she and her family were always neatly dressed, She was an excellent cook who could prepare healthful and palatable food with seemingly little effort.

There was very little farming in the community at that time. People had ranches and mostly sheep and cattle — mainly sheep in this part of the country. Most of the residents had been drawn into the country because land was cheap and wool prices high.

With the large comfortable house we had, it was possible to entertain visitors. The first ones to come were Uncle John Romberg and his wife, who had lately married. The relation between the two brothers had always been very harmonious so it was natural that the visitors made our home their headquarters and that we visited much with them as we all went around to the different relatives. After that, Grandmother and Grandfather Romberg and Aunt Ida came for an extended visit; and I had the opportunity of getting well acquainted with them. Since Grandfather had poor eyes, Grandmother read a great deal to him. It was sometimes difficult to find enough reading material. She also helped in the garden and in the house. Two of Aunt Louise's boys came over every day to receive help in arithmetic. Grandmother enjoyed instructing them, for she had been a teacher before her marriage and during pioneer days.

Later, in the fall of the year my father came in a new top buggy with instructions from my mother to bring me home, for she was anxious to see the baby. I was of course glad to go. I had expected this trip in a buggy to be easier, but the weather was hot and the roads were still rough. I still remember vividly the long stretch of road down through the cedar brakes to the crossing of the Colorado at Smithwick's Mill. And going up was still worse. Father walked all the way down and up to make it easier for the horse. I drove and. held the baby. The

river was said to be comparatively shallow at this crossing, but still the water went to the hubs. We drove that
night until the moon was up before we found a suitable
stopping place, which was with a very kind and pleasant widow lady and her daughter. The baby had a long
cry that night before he went to sleep. Father wanted me
to have some rest—for I was very, very tired, having
been in that buggy all day. So he took the little fellow
outside and walked up and down with him. The rest of
the journey was a little easier; but I realize now, when I
look back that the trip for two and one-half days was
very strenuous for a little boy five or six months old. In
Belton the baby was petted a great deal and, I am afraid,
was badly spoiled. After three weeks, your father came
to take us back home. I never did like to stay away from
him too long.

The year 1879 passed without any unusual happenings. Life was agreeable and easy and not lacking in social contacts. The men had a target club and met once a
month at Cypress Mill or at their club house at Shovel
Mount or at the private home of one or the other older
families that had roomy houses. Generally dinner or
supper or both were served. Everybody came, old and
young; and those that came from a farther distance spent
the night. The families that attended these gatherings
were not numerous and most of them were somewhat
related. They were mainly the families of Wilhelm
Fuchs, Fritz Fuchs, Goeth, Struve, Giesecke, Varnhagen,
Richter, Schroeter, Goebel, Ebeling and others. These
people loved music—and a good many had musical instruments, such as pianos and violins, in their homes. I
remember that we danced to music of several instruments, piano, violin, and cello, together. In the course of
time, we twice invited our friends for such a gathering.

Many of our friends, especially the older persons,
were well read and had good books—mostly the clas-

sics. To provide more reading material Mr. Alois Goebel promoted the idea of establishing a reading circle in the Cypress community. All readily joined by donating a small sum for the purchase of books, and your father was chosen as librarian. Most of the reading material was fiction, but there were also books on history, science and travel. This reading had an intellectually stimulating influence and furnished topics for conversation and discussion. When the organization was finally dissolved, the books were divided among the members. Of these books we still have in our library two illustrated volumes on Rome, two on Hellas and others.

By this time we had our own flock of sheep and kept a shepherd who lived with his family in one of the tenant houses. Most of the time Father also kept a hired hand to attend to the farm land, which was not rented out any more. As there was plenty to look after on the place, Father gave up the teaching.

In the spring of 1880 my mother finally came for a longer visit. Brother Bernhard, who was then seventeen, brought her in the buggy. Our house was just below a little elevation on the little Cypress. As the two approached our farm in the dark, they suddenly came to a short, steep bank. Because of the tracks of many sheep, no road was visible; and there was no other sign of human habitation. So they decided that they had lost the road and that it would be best to sit out a chilly night right there in the buggy. Next morning when our men folks were out very early, they discovered just below our hill, within calling distance of our house, this buggy and the two tired travelers. I certainly was surprised when Father brought them to me in the warm kitchen, where I was preparing breakfast.

Mother stayed with us about five weeks. During this time on Otto's birthday our first little daughter arrived [March 30, 1880], whom I wanted to name after my mother. However, Mother objected to the name, and so I used both my sister's and my mother's name for little Annie Auguste. It was certainly nice to have such a long visit from my mother, and I think she enjoyed it very much.

Next spring [1881] brother Louis, then about fifteen, but small for his age, came to help during the lambing season and to get acquainted with country life. Later he attended our school. Father could not praise enough this dependable, practical helper. Louis had really never known little children and played a great deal with our two now. He was much company to me, and I enjoyed his sense of humor. On the other hand, I think the change to country life, the higher altitude, were beneficial to his physical development.

I made two rugs and crocheted a table cover, which he was to take along for Mother. On the latter I worked constantly every spare minute in the last few days in order to get it finished. Father took him as far as Austin. While changing conveyances somewhere on the latter part of the way home, in the excitement of the first trip, he forgot his bag; and the articles that I had constructed with the idea of giving my mother a great deal of pleasure were lost and never recovered.

Next year Aunty Friederike Perlitz and Uncle Carl moved to a ranch seven miles below Cypress Mill, which they had bought and improved. Since Grandfather and Grandmother Romberg now had four married children in this vicinity, they came up the next summer for a lengthy visit. In this year our second little girl arrived [March 27, 1882]. This time Father suggested that we name her Ida after his dear sister Ida.

We had here on the Cypress certainly a pleasant mode of living and an interesting environment. All this was, however, really just a background for our chief interest, our children.

The Children

We now had quite a little family, and our greatest joy was the progress of our children. They were sweet, pretty and bright. We were very anxious to bring them up properly and to promote their physical development. It came in handy now that we knew two languages; for then when problems connected with the children arose, we could talk them over without the children understanding. We were both opposed to slapping and whipping and tried to solve our problems in a better way. Of course the children would get into all kinds of mischief like active children will.

One time when the children were alone in the house, I heard Annie crying pitifully. She was then in the crawling age. I hurried into the house, and there was my little Annie crawling on the floor toward the front door and Otto trotting back and forth, industriously carrying ashes in the shovel from the fireplace and pouring them on her back. Fortunately there had not been any fire since the night before, so the ashes were fairly cool. I hurriedly rescued my little girl and took off her clothes. I noticed a few little holes scorched into her dress; but since the dress was of woolen material, the incident did not harm her.

One day Father came home with a little puppy, declaring that our baby boy needed a playmate. Really, Otto and the dog grew up together and were constant companions. The dog, a long-haired shepherd, was called Watch; and to this day we have had a Watch in our family whenever there was a dog on the place, named after this especially smart and faithful shepherd dog. Otto was a strong child and learned to walk early. Children of this age have the habit of rambling off when by themselves. One day I missed my little boy; and after hunting for him all over the place I was sure that he had rambled into the pasture which joined our yard. This pasture was mainly used for calves and was densely wooded. I soon found his little tracks on a trail and heard a sheep bell that he usually played with, hanging it around his neck and trotting around to make it jingle. By this bell I soon found him. The dog was his companion, and would no doubt have taken care of him.

Another time when I missed little Otto—although I tried to watch him carefully—I tracked him down the road, saw where he had crawled through under a big gate out into the open range. His tracks went along the fence where a trail was. I certainly was glad when in the distance I saw Watch sitting by the fence, for I knew he would protect the little fellow. When I arrived the boy was on his "tummy" with his head through the fence, asleep. Of course he had cried, not being able to get his body through or his head back. I soon managed to get him out of the fence and carried him home.

Later, when Annie was old enough to run around, the children were one day playing in front of the house, where I heard Otto hammering very diligently. Then I heard Annie crying out aloud. I was sure he had mashed her finger. I dashed out and saw my little Annie standing there crying and some blood at one eye. I saw that Otto had been crushing glass, so I was scared that some had gotten into the eye. Holding her tight, I managed to open her eye and found a small piece of glass in the corner of the eye, where it had made a cut. How easily the child could have impaired her eyesight.

Once Annie had stuck a pea into her nose, which I could not remove. I got Father's tobacco pouch, held it to her nose to make her sneeze, and out came the pea.

Once when I missed the children and went out to look for them, they were on the high roof of an old barn.

The front of this barn was very high and the roof had a depression on which were old cans and horse shoes, which boys may have thrown up there. The two children were sitting up there and examining these valuables. Speaking to them calmly, I walked up to the back of the shed where they had managed to climb up over the long sloping roof of the sheep shed and where it was easy to get them down again. This escapade was never repeated

Another time when it was so unusually quiet that I suspected the children in some mischief, I looked for them everywhere I could think of! But I could not find them. I looked into the smokehouse in a hurry as I passed by, thinking they could have gone to sleep. Finally I looked into the smokehouse once more, because it was somewhat dark in there; and I noticed my two children sitting very quietly near the wine barrel. Father had made a barrel of wine this year, which was now in the stage where it was tested by sucking up some of it with a cane tube to see whether it was ready to seal. Otto had no doubt seen this performance, and he and Annie tried it also. As they looked so ill, I was worried about the consequences the drinking of this strong stuff might have. Annie soon vomited up her portion and then quietly went to sleep. But Otto got funny and foolish and was no doubt a little drunk. Later on he also went to sleep, and Father saw to it that the barrel was permanently closed.

Later on when the children were old enough to help me, one day when I was washing, I had them help hanging up the small pieces, which we generally spread on low bushes that were close by. When I later passed, I noticed with dismay that the children had spread a good many of the clothes on big cactus leaves. No one can imagine what work I had to remove these small stickers that covered some pieces, and in spite of my care there were complaints later on when a sticker had worked itself into the skin.

I was always in favor of having little family festivities, celebrating Christmas, birthdays and the like. For the first few years we spent Christmas evening with Aunt Louise; but when Otto was just a little tot, I decided that he should be surprised with his own Christmas tree. With great secrecy I made a lot of preparation. One day when I was baking little animal cookies, little Otto must have noticed the oven door slamming occasionally. When I had been out of the room and was returning, he was holding open the oven door and calling out, "This is a nice horsey."

After Otto got older the children were less trouble as he was a smart sensible boy, who helped to take care of the rest.

On the Romberg Ranch

In 1882 we sold the Cleveland place and bought instead Uncle Carl Perlitz' ranch which was on the Cypress Creek seven miles below Cypress Mill. This place was from then on generally known as the Romberg ranch. There were several reasons for moving to the new place. The country was settling up and fenced in very fast; and Father was afraid that we soon would not have enough range on the Cleveland place, which comprised only some seven hundred acres, while the new one had over two thousand. Then Uncle Carl was very much dissatisfied with ranch life and wanted to sell out. Besides, Uncle John had ready money which he wanted to invest in the sheep business, which was very profitable then. So he and Father together bought the ranch, which was to be under Father's management.

Since I was leaving so many good friends and near neighbors at Cypress Mill, I thought life would be very lonesome on the new ranch. However, in the beginning we lived for two months in the same house with Aunt Friederike before she moved and this arrangement made our life full and interesting. I got well acquainted with Aunt Friederike, her seven young daughters and one little baby boy — Erich.

Then when they left, we bought their piano, which gave us much entertainment, especially in the winter. I started to practice again to be able to accompany Father with the violin. We got much enjoyment out of our music. The Strauss waltzes were particularly popular then.

We also had much company at times. Our friends did not mind coming the extra distance. Sister Anna and brother Bernhard came and some of the kinfolks from Fayette County. Then

I also went to Belton with my three children for a two weeks' visit.

This time we were to go over Austin, 35 miles away, and from there to take the train. After we had driven nearly all day, we camped out near Austin. About noon next day Father put us on the train and started home again. When he reached the other side of the Colorado, which had no bridge at that time, there was old Watch. We had left him tied at home, and the shepherd must have untied him at night. That faithful dog was very much attached to the children; and missing them, he must have tracked us all night those thirty-five miles to Austin until the river stopped him.

I had always wanted to have pictures taken of the children. On my visit to Belton, I had the first opportunity to have this done. For many years, I have treasured those photographs; and I still get them out now and then to enjoy them.

In the fall of 1885 our second little boy was born [November 15, 1884?]. I wanted to name him Julius, but Father objected and suggested that we name him Hermann after Uncle Hermann Bauch, a kind and gentle person that Father had always loved and admired. And so we called our boy Hermann Julius. I have always felt that naming a child after a good person was like giving that child a good start in life, that somehow the good character traits would later develop in the child also. In this particular case, my premonition proved true.

Our ranch life had many interesting aspects. Father was still young then and liked to go hunting. His well-trained dog, Watch, would go out by himself at night and tree some wild animal. He would stay there and bark until Father came — no matter how cold and disagreeable the night — to shoot the varmint and bring the dog back home. When he first moved to our new ranch, Watch in a short time treed fifteen foxes, besides raccoons and opossums. No wonder that Aunt Friederike could not raise any chickens.

One day the children, playing in front of the house, reported a "big animal." On looking out, I saw a wildcat walking leisurely almost through our front yard and then on toward the branch. Father and Uncle Bennie Fuchs, who happened to be there and who was a great hunter, rushed excitedly after with dog and gun, but the wildcat had evidently gone somewhere across the Cypress.

One night, when we were still living on the Cleveland place, we heard an unfamiliar, weird cry, and Father decided that it must be a wildcat, perhaps in one of the big cypress trees. Such an animal could be very destructive to our herd of sheep and had to be killed if possible. The gun was brought out, but there were no bullets. In those days bullets were molded at home by pouring molten lead into an instrument about the size of fence pliers. This instrument was known as a bullet mold. Well, Father and the shepherd both got busy; but by the time they were ready with their gun, the weird cry and the animal were gone. Later Uncle Bennie told us that we had heard the screech of a certain large owl.

Ranch life had its humorous aspects. When we still lived on the Cleveland place and brother Louis was with us, we had among a herd of rams one cantankerous animal that never gave any trouble to Father but insisted on butting brother Louis every time the opportunity presented itself — unexpectedly, if possible. Louis did not dare to be in an open place with the ram around. Hot-headed Louis would have enjoyed chastising the ram; but such an animal is very well protected by a heavy pelt and the head is very hard. It was impossible to whip or spank the ram. The only thing Louis could do was to grab the animal by a horn and to lead him to a place from where escape was possible.

One night when Father was not at home, this malicious ram had butted down the yard gate and walked into the open hall of the house to scratch around in front of Louis' door. To chase him away, I opened my door on the opposite side of the hall and pitched a shoe at him. The animal then turned around and fussed at my door. It was Louis' time to land a bootjack. But the ram could not be induced by any such means to leave the house. Finally brother Louis caught him by a horn, we led him out, and tied the gate up well with rope.

One afternoon Father heard from the house a call of "Youhoo" in the distance. "It's brother John's voice," he said excitedly. "Where in the world is he coming from and why this call?" Father went out immediately to search, guided by the calls that were repeated at intervals; and found short, plump Uncle John perched on a skinny mesquite tree with the ram standing beneath. Uncle John had come to Cypress Mill and had decided to surprise us. As he was walking peacefully through the pasture, the ram suddenly butted him from behind, retreated for another running start and butted again, so that Uncle John was finally forced to find safety in the tree. His good voice helped him out of the difficulty.

A great objection to the new ranch was that it was too lonesome. We had no real neighbors. I was always a very healthy person, but it happened twice on this place that Father after having been away all day, came home to find me sick in bed. One time when a norther had set in and it was getting cold for the children, I told Otto from my bed how to build a fire in the cook stove to warm up the room. I thought he was perfectly capable to do this, for he was a bright boy and had seen many times how it was done. Father arrived just as that child was ready to strike a match. He was very much disturbed, for he was always very much afraid of fire.

To avoid another situation like the one just related Father thought of moving his family to a more settled community and to start teaching again. A circumstance that made it easier for us to come to such a decision was the fact that the sheep business, which had always given us a good income, had declined until it did not pay very well. The drop in the price of wool was due to the fact that the federal government lifted the tariff on wool, and so foreign wool was imported freely. However, the deciding factor in making the change was the hope of giving our children a better opportunity for education and progress. When Father was offered a good teaching position in a rural school in Fayette County, we put our shepherd, who had been with us for several years, in charge of the ranch and moved. To this day I think we made a very wise decision when we chose a different environment for bringing up our children

Our relatives and friends were sorry to see us go and arranged a big picnic for the day of our departure. The picnic was below the bluffs of the Cypress in a cool and shady place. Everybody came from far and near to tell us good-bye. When all the picnickers had gone again, we also left to get a good start on our way to Austin. With the good wishes of our friends in our minds, it was not so difficult to leave.

We moved away in August of 1885. We sold the sheep and cattle after a few years and just rented out the ranch. Although we lived on this place only three years, we kept the ranch for fifty years and finally sold it in June, 1935.

Four Years at O'Quinn

Father made several trips to bring our household goods from the ranch to Fayette County. In the meantime the children and I had gone by train from Austin to San Antonio, to which place my family had moved a short time before. I stayed there about two weeks and then went by train to Fayette County, where I stayed with Aunt Bernhardine until the new house which the farmers at O'Quinn were building for us was ready. We moved into this new home on October 17, 1885.

Our new home was in an environment very different from the one we had left in Blanco County. We were in a thickly settled community, one of the oldest in Texas. The country was rolling prairie. All around us were close neighbors, farmers who owned their homes, worked hard and prospered. They were Industrious, helpful, kind, thrifty, ready to assist in community undertakings. Their homes were usually on a little hill; the residences were painted white and surrounded with a grove of planted. trees. They usually had a big barn and other improvements, and generally a row of hay stacks for winter feeding. They planted cotton and corn and had some cattle. Altogether they were well off, and theirs was a very normal and healthy life. There was still a lot of pasture all around us with the original Texas prairie grass, tall and thrifty.

We had a nice family life, for Father was always around home and not gone all day, as was frequently the case on the ranch. Our house was right by the school yard, and Father could come home for his meals. We had been told that some of the pupils had been very unruly and that some of the big boys had been whipped every day. Although Father had between forty and fifty students, he never whipped a single boy in all the four years he was there. No punishment was necessary. There was order and a friendly spirit in the school room. To get exercise and to keep an eye on the children, Father played with them during the intermissions baseball, last lick and anti-over. In the evening before he dismissed them, he let the children sing while he played the violin so that they were in a happy spirit when they left.

In the fall and winter when the school was crowded, I sometimes helped to teach the smaller children, of whom I had several at a time. The children liked this. The exercise of running back and forth from the school to our house was good for them. They were good children, and I enjoyed the teaching. At the request of some of the neighbors Father had a night school part of the time for a class of young men. After school he gave at times violin lessons.

The school building was quite roomy, so it was used for all sorts of community affairs. Father went to these gatherings, and the neighbors soon relied upon him for leadership. The building was used by the young folks for parties and dances — with the parents present to look on. The women brought their little ones over to our house and put them on a bed or pallet to sleep. Then these women either went back to the festivity or they chatted with me. They were friendly and social

Twice we went to a big wedding in this community. One went in the afternoon for the wedding ceremony and later had supper in a long arbor, which was especially built for the occasion and which contained tables covered with good things to eat. The occasion closed with a dance at night. Everybody enjoyed these weddings and talked about them long before and after. Only the nearest friends would give presents — a few inexpensive, practical presents.

I always enjoyed doing fancy work, for it was restful. Besides, I enjoyed decorating my house with such things as a crocheted table cover, an embroidered pillow or dresser scarf. I also liked to trim the children's clothes with homemade laces as was fashionable then. My fancy work was always admired by the ladies in the neighborhood. When they expressed the desire that I would help their girls to learn how to do this, I talked it over with Father; and we decided to set aside Friday afternoon for this instruction, which I gave in my own house for girls that were interested. It was a pleasure for me to help them, for they were so anxious to learn and enjoyed it so much. Besides, these good neighbors were always doing something for us — bringing us fresh sausage and spare ribs during the hog-killing season and perhaps another time a sample of their new supply of homemade sorghum molasses, which they knew so well how to make.

Another thing we liked about our home in O'Quinn was that we were living within easy visiting distance of our relatives. The Romberg kinfolks lived only four miles away. One or the other would come for us on Friday afternoon and bring us back Sunday evening. Grandfather Mackensen and Aunt Anna came by train; and quite often we saw brother Bernhard, who was teaching in the vicinity. Once during a vacation, we went by hack to the Ohlendorfs and Roeders[5]. The latter had a

5   Von Roeder. The largest of contingent of the Cat Spring pioneers was the extended family of Ludwig Sigismund Anton von Roeder. They had read Ernst's letter and decided to make the move. Initially four unmarried children of Ludwig von Roeder (Albrecht, Ludwig / Louis, Joachim and Valeska) and a servant named Franz Pollhart were sent in early 1834 to scout the territory and begin planning for the rest of the family to join them. Traveling with them was a couple from Canton Aargau, Switzerland, Charles and Mary Amsler. All initially proceeded to the Industry settlement of Ernst and Fortran, but soon selected their land grants on the Gotier Trace about half way between San Felipe and Industry. Here, soon after they arrived, Louis von Roeder killed a "wild cat" (probably a bobcat) at a nearby spring and thus the settlement was named "katzen-

house full of children like we had, and these youngsters
played well together.

Mr. Roeder, like Father, was still teaching. This trip
now took us only one day.

We lived in this O'Quinn community four years.
Once more the whole family was happy over the arrival
of a little baby [July 1, 1887]. This time the little girl was
named after grandmother Romberg and Aunt Louise.
She was our Frederica Louise.

It was nice to have our relatives so close by for joyful
gatherings. In time of sickness and sorrow, they were
also there with help and consolation. During the spring
of our first year at O'Quinn, I went to San Antonio
where Aunt Joline [Caroline Buehring Romberg, wife of
Uncle John (Johannes) Romberg] was recuperating at the
home of my father from an operation. While I was helping to nurse her, the children were staying with Aunt
Ida. Father got sick and wrote that he would love to see
me back again as he was feeling very ill. I was shocked
when I saw how helpless he was. The doctor said he had
inflammatory rheumatism. It was fortunate that he was
at Uncle John's where both Uncle John and Uncle Bernhard could help nurse—especially when the hot baths
had to be given with frequent reference to the clock and
thermometer. Bath tubs and hot water installation were
unknown in those days. Fortunately there was a large
bathing vat in the family, made of tin with a wooden
bottom, and long enough that Father could be entirely
submerged. He read to be lifted in and out because he
was perfectly helpless. It was so painful for him to lie
down that he had to sit up most of the time. Since he

---

quelle", or Cat Spring. Into the 1850s it was referred to as "Wild Cat
Spring". (ibid. p. 16). Caroline von Roeder married Ferdinand Engelking
after he arrived in Texas. These families came from the area around Min-
den in Germany. More information can be found in "The Engelking Letters" by Flora von Roeder and about the Sack Family to which they are
connected in a number of publications from this house.

could not move sufficiently for us to dress him, we wrapped. him up in woolen blankets and cloths. These cloths had to be frequently changed day and night when they became damp of excessive perspiration. After several weeks his condition improved, and finally we were able to go back to our home, where Father had to resume his teaching. It took years for him to get entirely over the effects of this serious illness.

The last winter of our stay at O'Quinn was warm and very wet, and this condition probably caused lots of sickness in the coming spring. Our children got ill, especially little Frederica was sick. When Otto got sick, the doctor declared he had typhoid. We were very much worried when we heard this, for there was much typhoid in the country and most cases were virulent; but Otto always had been such a strong, healthy boy that we hoped he would pull through. But he died on the seventh day of his illness [April 1, 1889].

After this Uncle John took the family over to his house to stay a while. In the meantime Father went to the ranch on business. Before his return all the children had taken the whooping cough, which was also very severe that year. With Father's return, we went back home so that Father could resume his teaching; but now I fell ill and was in bed a week or two. Aunt Ida came over and took care of the family.

That summer we decided to leave the place where we had had so much trouble, and to move to the Romberg neighborhood. All of Father's family were very much in favor of this change. They needed a school in their community and thought Father might as well be teaching there. Besides, with the help of a hired hand, Father could combine farming with his teaching, which would be much better for his health than the steady teaching he had been doing. And so we moved in the fall of 1889 to a little farm owned by Aunt Ida, which was only a half mile from Uncle John's house.

After we were well established in our new home, Father opened up a new school which was attended very enthusiastically by our children, a number of their cousins and also the children of some nearby families that were not relatives.

Everything was much better in this new environment except the house in which we lived. I decided that that was after all of minor importance.

Grandfather Romberg And His Family
At Black Jack Springs

As we lived for nine years in the Romberg community (1889-1898) and as during that time we were intimately associated with Father's brothers and sisters, I shall try to give a clear picture of them; for these good people influenced the thinking, helped to mold the character and established the outlook on life of our older children. I would like for these younger ones, who have never known any of these good uncles and aunts personally, to know something about them and to appreciate them, too.

Grandfather Romberg was very highly pleased to have his youngest son back in the old surroundings. When the weather permitted Grandfather, with a cane and a little bag containing the mail, would go around to the homes of his different children. There was much mail received in this family; besides, papers and magazines were passed around so all could read them. The weather never was too warm for Grandfather, so it seemed. He distributed the mail to make himself useful, to have exercise and to have the contacts with his children. He was a small man and still very straight. He liked a good conversation, an interesting discussion, kindly humor; and was especially pleased when he could play a game of chess with a good antagonist. Uncle Hermann Bauch, Uncle John and Father played mostly with him.

He came to Texas, to Cat Spring, with his family in 1847; and in 1853 moved to Fayette County to the place where he lived from then on. After Grandmother's death in 1882, Aunt Ida cared for him very faithfully. As his eyesight was impaired, Uncle John and Aunt Joline read a great deal to him. He was, therefore, well informed about current affairs. Up to his death at the age of eighty-four, he considered himself very fortunate to have so many of his children and. grandchildren close by.

Of these children, his oldest daughter, Aunt Bernhardine Franke, lived about a quarter of a mile away. Her eight children had grown up right there on her place. When we moved into the community, the older children were already away from home. Some were married and lived nearby. Her youngest son, Hermann, we saw a great deal, though he did not attend our school anymore.

Uncle Bernhard Romberg and Aunt Berline lived about half a mile in another direction from Grandfather's house. Helene, the oldest daughter, was already away from home; but the four boys were still in school; and the youngest, Arnold, was of Ida's age.

Uncle John Romberg had taken charge of Grandfather's place. He married late in life. He was short, plump, cheerful, wise, friendly, kindhearted, lovable. His wife, Aunt Joline, lived in Europe until she was in her thirties. She was therefore well educated, especially in music. She came to Texas to teach Aunt Louise's children; but stopping first with her aunt, who was Grandmother Romberg, she was so pleased with her reception that she accepted a position with her cousin, Aunt Bernhardine, to teach the children. It was not long before she and Uncle John were married, and it was a very happy union. Their children, Walter and Hedwig, were of the age of Annie and Ida, and theirs the second home of our children.

Aunt Ida never married and always lived with Uncle John's family, helping to rear the children as their mother was much in delicate health. This good Aunt Ida was really the mother of the whole community.

A peculiar situation in this Romberg family was that there were three Aunt Carolines. It was Grandfather Romberg who suggested adding the first syllable of the husband's name for distinction. Uncle Bernhard's wife Aunt Berline, pronounced in three syllables, Ber-lee-ne; Uncle John's wife was Aunt Joline; and I was Aunt Juline (Ju-lee-ne). To avoid confusion these names were always used.

To me the four aunts who all lived within walking distance were like sisters. Almost every day I saw one or the other of them, and we talked over our problems. I appreciated their advice and valued their judgment. Between us there was complete harmony and understanding.

These four aunts were intimately known and loved by our children; and therefore the maturer minds easily exerted a guiding influence over the young impressionable ones.

It gives me pleasure to think of these women and to recall here incidents of my life connected with them.

Aunt Ida

Of all the relatives none was loved more than Aunt Ida. Since she never married, she kept house for her aged parents and for Uncle John and looked after all of them and others of the kinfolks who had trouble. When Uncle John married, the household continued in the old way. Aunt Ida looked after the household duties as before. Later when the little children — Walter and Hedwig — came, she had them under her care, for the mother was often sickly; besides she was inexperienced in household duties and very short sighted. Aunt Caroline's attempts at housekeeping were a misfortune — despite her efforts. So it was natural that in the course of years Aunt Ida took over the entire responsibility for housekeeping in that home.

To the two children Aunt Ida was a second mother. They went to her for consolation and help in all of their little sorrows, aches and pains. And for Aunt Ida life was made rich and happy with these duties. She never complained. Whenever there was sickness in the family and help needed, Aunt Ida would assist. At times our family would have been in distress had not Aunt Ida helped out in her quiet, friendly and efficient way. In later years, too, her nieces and nephews came back to her for advice. She had the rare gift to find easily the right solution for their problems. Long after we had moved away from Black Jack Springs, the small children in our family still received by mail toys at Christmas time; and in her will she left her property to all her nieces and nephews — which was a final evidence of her devotion to the children of her big family.

Social Life in the Romberg Community

Aunt Joline contributed much to the social life of the community. She had time for this because Aunt Ida attended to the household duties. She was well educated and continued to find time to read.. Having always lived in large cities before she came to Texas, she had met interesting people. Everybody liked to be in her company because she was entertaining. She was a good conversationalist and could tell any little incident in an interesting manner.

Then Aunt Joline was an excellent musician. She played the piano with great skill and also had a well-trained voice. She gladly contributed suitable music to any of our gatherings, taught the children how to play the piano and how to sing and accompanied them with ease and with pleasure.

She had a distinguished appearance and moved with poise in any social gathering. However, she was almost at a loss when left alone to entertain a plain farm woman. Somehow she always met interesting and cultured people whom she invited for a visit in her home. She did this because she liked to entertain, and because these visitors brought a change into our quiet country life. It was Aunt Joline who instigated occasional theatricals. For Grandfather's and for Uncle John's birthdays and for New Year's night she practiced with the children little plays. She found time to select suitable plays to plan and arrange costumes, decorations, stage and curtains. Soon all of us were enthusiastic helpers. Our girls always took part in the performances and learned to act before an audience—which consisted of all the kinfolks and intimate friends, young and old.

These affairs were staged in Uncle John's large hall, open on the south and closed on the north side. The north end with its many exits was very well suited for a stage.

My part of the help usually consisted in preparing the costumes according to Aunt Joline's directions. I prepared angel wings, crowns, trains, peasant costumes and so on. Or I helped with the singing behind the scenes. And between the acts I helped with the changing of the costumes. All this was a great pleasure to me, though it required much time and work.

To Aunt Joline no play—nor any other social gathering—was complete without music. She could select the right music for each occasion and enjoyed training singers and performers on instruments.

It was fortunate that there was in the Romberg family one person who had the time, the inclination and ability to undertake such social activities, so stimulating to all. Her influence helped to make life very different from what it is in most rural communities.

Aunt Joline loved children, and our children were all very fond of her and were therefore easily influenced by this talented and interesting aunt.

Yes, Aunt Joline contributed much to the social life in our community.

I remember well how heartily I was received by Aunt Berline whenever I appeared with my little flock at her front gate. She was usually occupied in the large hall— open on the south—of her spacious home and came gracefully and quickly without haste, to meet us at the gate. She gave me both her hands cordially, received me gladly, and had a happy greeting for each child—all of which made us feel very welcome.

She was a good housekeeper. Not strong, she planned so well that she finished her household duties in the most efficient way without ever rushing.

She saw to it that at every family gathering there was an interesting conversation. She read much in order to stimulate such a conversation. She was aided in this by her excellent memory. She could read a poem through a few times and then would know it by heart. And she could write very beautiful poems herself.

Uncle Bernhard was a deep thinker and always ready to take part in a discussion, but she was the one that brought up the topics that were suitable for general discussion. She did this in a larger group, and she did this every day at home at the dinner table.

As her children were growing up and needed some social life, she organized a literary society at which she presided. This organization flourished especially during the summer months. She was interested in giving her boys and the other young folks an opportunity to practice speaking before an audience. Father took a very active part in the programs, and so did Uncle Bernhard and the older cousins who were home from college or from their teaching. Even the children participated. Mostly these recited a poem or took part in a dialog or they sang a song. Then they ran off to play outside while the older ones took up an assigned topic for discussion. Perhaps the older children would stay and listen a while. Very frequently there was a debate—with judges to render a decision later. Usually the subject was assigned to definite speakers who were prepared. After these finished everybody who wanted to could contribute facts or opinions. I remember such questions as "What is character?" "Who was the best president?" In this informal organization all were encouraged to contribute whatever they wanted.

The meetings were held at the different homes and always on Sunday afternoons. Coffee and cake were served. Everybody departed with the feeling of having spent a pleasant and enjoyable afternoon. One summer when we were starting these meetings again, everybody was to suggest a name for the organization. Many beautiful and suitable names were submitted. Finally Father suggested to name it the Opossum as the organization usually died down in the winter and then came to life in the next summer. This name seemed very appropriate, and it stuck. For years then our family attended the Opossum.

Also within a mile from our house lived white-haired Uncle Hermann Bauch, the youngest brother of Grandmother Romberg, and our equally white-haired Aunt Erna, two dear people in a cozy home. These two had married late in life and adopted a little boy to whom they were devoted. Their house was painted white and had green shutters and trimmings; the yard fence was also painted white and surrounded the shaded yard. Everybody liked to go to this home, for no one knew better how to entertain guests than these two old experienced and well-read people. Aunt Erna's excellent coffee was served in quaint china cups, and her cake was served on antique plates. There were silver spoons of ancient design, and a beautiful old linen table cover was spread over the round table that always stood in front of the sofa. Over the table was the hanging lamp, with its shade fringed with glass tassels, always very much admired by the youngsters. The windows had snowy curtains, and on the walls were old-fashioned pictures. Aunt Erna presided at her coffee table with much dignity. She always looked like a distinguished lady. And Uncle Hermann knew how to keep the conversation going. One always spent very pleasant hours with these two old people in their cozy home. They subscribed to some very good illustrated German magazines, and they passed these on to other homes. The discussion of the continued stories or of the articles in those magazines formed part of the conversation at such a visit.

It was with pleasure that these two gave to the three girls, Annie, Ida, and Hedwig, the subscription to a very excellent illustrated magazine for girls. We still have whole sets of these magazines in our library. They were later read by our younger girls, and I have also read them to my grandchildren.

The celebration of the silver wedding anniversary of Uncle Hermann and Aunt Erna was a great event. Relatives from our community and from a distance attended. Aunt Joline was glad to have an opportunity of exercising her ability to provide the proper music and theatrical performances for this occasion. She induced Professor Sibberns, a music critic from Vienna, visiting at that time at Uncle John's, to write a longer play—in verse—which was based on the life of Uncle Hermann and Aunt Erna. Of course there was a big dinner and equally sumptuous supper. And in the afternoon ice cream was served. It was the first time this delicacy had been served in this community. It was something new and something extra.

Social life was also stimulated because of interesting visitors. In our family the folks from San Antonio visited for weeks at a time.

Since we lived in the same house with Aunt Bernhardine for four years, I will write more in detail about this ambitious family later. However, I want to mention here their contribution to our social life. Since Aunt Bernhardine was the oldest one of Grandfather Romberg's children, all the Franke cousins were grown when we lived at Black Jack Springs. When these cousins were at home for vacations and visits, they took a lively interest in the literary society. They were especially good in debate.

As the children in the other families grew up and went off to school, they, too, came back with new ideas for discussions.

Our sojourn and activities in this community for twelve years had a permanent influence on our daily life, our interests and our plans for the children.

At Aunt Bernhardine's

We had lived on Aunt Ida's place for one year when Aunt Bernhardine suggested we move to her more spacious home and take charge of her much larger fields. This suggestion she made because she was alone with her youngest son, Hermann; and he was sickly at that time. She could use the five upstairs rooms, and we could use the six downstairs. We made the change in the fall of 1890 and were always glad we had done so, for life on her place had many interesting features.

Aunt Bernhardine was the oldest one of Grandfather Romberg's children. She married at eighteen and lived first in Independence, where her husband was a teacher of music in Baylor College. Because there was too much malaria in Independence, they moved back to Fayette County, where she lived many years within half a mile of her parents. Part of the time her husband was away from home because the doctors advised him to go north and later because he was legislator in Austin. He died suddenly while in Austin when her youngest child was six weeks old and her oldest eighteen. Since that time Aunt Bernhardine had had the entire responsibility of bringing up her eight children.

She took this responsibility very seriously, keeping the children away from possible country entertainments, and seeing to it that they attended church. Her children were hard-working, dependable, studious and ambitious. While they had to attend to their farm duties, they studied a great deal at home. Four of her children went north for a while to study; and later her youngest son, Hermann, went to the University of Texas to study law. Since the income at home was not such that they could all be supported in school, they had to work first to earn sufficient money to continue their studies. Several of them had the musical talent of their father.

Aunt Bernhardine was intelligent, capable and practical. The many responsibilities she had to assume early in her life made her appear a little bit stern. But she was very kind and helpful. This I know because I lived in the house with her for several years.

Aunt Bernhardine had a really beautiful farm home. She had a roomy two-story house, painted white. The grape vine that ran up to the second story of the portico was very picturesque, and the broad stone steps in front of the house were equally imposing. In front of the house was a lawn enclosed by a trimmed hedge, and beyond the hedge was a grass meadow of several acres, where our children used to play and gather flowers. Beyond all this were a pasture with trees and the Navidad, which started as a creek at the Black Jack Springs in Aunt Bernhardine's pasture. On the right side of the meadow was a beautiful grove of live-oaks and around the house were more live-oaks. The children played under these trees and climbed around in them to their heart's content. Toward the rear of the residence were a number of barns, because this used to be a large farm and much cattle was once raised here, too. The place was a regular paradise for children. They swung in the trees, played in the hayloft, waded in the creek and rode the old farm horse.

I also liked Aunt Bernhardine's place. The house had been lived in for a long time and had been conveniently arranged, which made housekeeping easy. Aunt Bernhardine helped out in a pinch. It was entertaining to me to live in the house with her, for we had many interests in common. She was much older and more experienced and there was lots I could learn from her, which I was very glad to do.

Father managed the farm and continued his teaching. The children had to pass Uncle John's house on their way to school; so they stopped there for Walter and Hedwig, or they played there a while on the way back from school. Hardly a day passed that the three girls were not there. And Father stopped for a chat with Uncle John.

Whenever Aunt Bernhardine's children came home from their studies or their teaching or from trips, it was interesting to listen to their descriptions of what they had seen, heard and experienced. When they were at home, especially Louis and Marie practiced on the piano a great deal. Our children became familiar with good music; and even little Hermann, who had a good ear for music, would sing to himself Paderewsky's Minuet while he played.

Naturally our children received some petting from the cousins so much older. I remember well how a cruller or cookie attached to a thread dangled down from above until it was just within reach from our kitchen window, and Hermann and Frederica made grabs at the goodies that bobbed up and down mysteriously.

There was a single pecan tree on the meadow near the house. Here Aunt Bernhardine would ramble sometimes with Hermann and Frederica and find pecans in and out of season—pecans which she carried down in her pocket and dropped secretly for the delighted children.

We now had another fine little boy in our home. This time we named him Carl Bernhard [born June 19, 1890]. He was named after Uncle Carl Ohlendorf and after me. And both Father and I had a brother named Bernhard. When little Carl was about a year and a half old and good on his feet, he was inclined to run off. One day when we were all taking our afternoon nap, cousin

Marie called down from the portico, "Aunt Caroline, look out the window and see the spectacle." Out in the hot sun ran little Carl with somebody's big straw hat on and otherwise stark naked. He was trotting along a little trail in the meadow.

Another time he ran up to Uncle John's, and he was so far ahead of me that I never did catch up with him until he was nearly there. I followed with an umbrella because it was starting to rain. I had had the intention of whipping him to cure him of this habit of running off; but the heavy shower coming, I just picked up my boy and hurried to Uncle John's for shelter. The chastisement was omitted.

English walnuts were usually included among the Christmas goodies. One year little Hermann treasured some of them a while. Then one day he told me that he had planted one of these nuts. Some time later he reported that he had dug after the nut to see how it was getting along and found that it was heading downward. He had turned it around and hoped it would soon come up. I suppose that everybody knows that a nut develops its root first.

There were no darkeys in this country. The children did not know them. One afternoon I had sent Hermann and Frederica with a little lunch to carry to the other children. After a while I heard terrified screams from Frederica. I hurried out. The two children came running back home. Frederica was frightened to death. She was followed leisurely by a kindly, smiling Negro woman, black as night. The white teeth and eyeballs must have been the cause of the child's panic.

To learn how to ride, one has to know how to handle a horse. Ida was an expert handler of old Lolo, the patient family horse. After he had had his feed at noon, Ida was leader and Frederica as faithful attendant, would lead him a little distance away from the lot, climb on, and of course the horse, knowing where his dinner was served, walked back to the lot. Then they would lead him off again and repeat the performance. While he was walking back without any urging or managing on part of the children, they clung to him and to each other like burrs. If one lost her balance and slipped off, the other one went along, too. After several such expeditions, the old horse would get tired of the nuisance and would walk under low trees to scrape them off. For that day then the old animal had peace.

A patient horse in a family with many small children is an asset. One day I hitched up our old horse to drive with the babies to one of the aunts. It was Hermann Franke who came out that day to hitch the horse. I could see that he was highly amused about something. Finally he asked who had harnessed up the horse. I proudly said, "Oh, I did that myself this time." His smile spread. "It is lucky the horse is so gentle, or you might have had an accident. You put the collar on upside down."

On one side of Aunt Bernhardine's house was woodland. The children always enjoyed a stroll there, and I still have a little poem that Father made about a walk with our little bunch in these woods on a Sunday afternoon. I am going to include it in my story although there may be some in the family who cannot read it, for it is written in German.

One summer when the water in the cistern got very low, we did not want to exhaust the supply with big family washings. After much deliberation, we decided to perform this necessary task at the Black Jack Springs, up in the pasture. Father hitched up the wagon, put on the washing machine, the tubs and kettles; and everybody scrambled on. One of the larger girls had to stay at home to cook dinner, the other went along to take care of the baby and to watch the children while Father and I did the washing.

The children enjoyed such a wash day, for this was such a fine place to play. There were grapevines to swing on, clean sand to scratch around in, beautiful shade everywhere, and clear water for wading. For the children this was a real picnic. They were sorry when after a few weeks these excursions were not necessary anymore.

While we were living at Aunt Bernhardine's our fourth little girl arrived [December 13, 1892], and we named her after her two good aunts Erna Bernhardine. She was a very sweet little girl and adored by her big sisters — and everybody else. She had lots of pet names and was dainty and pretty as a doll. When playing alone she had a way of giggling to herself.

Yes, life at Aunt Bernhardine's place was very pleasant. However, she finally decided to sell the place and to move to El Campo, where several of her children lived. And so after four years we moved once more to Aunt Ida's place — which also had its charms and conveniences.

The Trip to the Wedding of Uncle Bernhard and Aunt Marie

While we were still living with Aunt Bernhardine, on August 3, 1891, my brother Bernhard and Marie Perlitz had their wedding. Aunt Ida and I—with the three youngest children—decided to enjoy this occasion. Annie and Ida were to stay at home and take care of the housekeeping—Aunt Bernhardine was there to consult. So one morning at daybreak, Father took us to West Point, the nearest railroad station, thirteen miles away, if one took a short route through the woods. This route Father hoped to find, but since we traveled on a small road, and since there were too many other small roads in the woods, we arrived at the station just as the train pulled out.

After much consideration we decided to remain at West Point—consisting of the station and a few scattered houses. There was no hotel, but an old couple that was running a restaurant was willing to let us have a small room. On account of the heat, we spent a very unpleasant day there and a much more unpleasant night. The three little ones just could not be made comfortable.

Next day we were at the station very early and glad when we were safely on the train. When we arrived at Coupland at noon—also a very small station—there was no one to meet us, and no conveyance of any kind to take us out to Uncle Carl's. A young man who owned a store and to whom we went for inquiries, offered to help us; and so we walked the one mile. One of us carried the baby, the other one helped the two children, and the young man carried the luggage. It was right after noon and fearfully hot, but we arrived safely and enjoyed a whole week's visit with our relatives.

Aunt Frederike's young girls, that we had known so well at the ranch, had grown up to fine young women. I had a real rest this week, although I assisted some with the wedding preparations. This was one of the most enjoyable weddings I ever attended.

The day before the wedding a number of guests arrived: Aunt Joline, Aunt Berline's boys, Helene, my sister Anna from San Antonio, Uncle Hermann and Aunt Herline and their girls from Burnet County.

The night before the wedding we had a *Polterabend*, a frolic in honor of the bride and groom. The sisters had secretly held rehearsals in the barn, or hurriedly finished costumes while the bride and groom were taking a walk. On this evening then, all young folks of the family and guests appeared as gypsies who set up camp in the big living room and presented the bride and groom with gifts, making in this connection suitable speeches of homemade verses — usually humorous. They sang and danced, read the happy and prosperous future of the bridal couple in cards, and finally broke camp and wandered on. There were a number of similar, suitable performances.

The wedding ceremony took place the next day. It was followed by a sumptuous dinner. We left the next evening, meeting Uncle John at West Point at sundown. It had rained heavily in the afternoon, the roads were bad, and we were crowded in the hack because Uncle Hermann and his family were with us, too. Driving was slow, and we had not proceeded very far before it got perfectly dark. Uncle Hermann walked in front carrying a lantern. As he was stepping along in the mud, he sang a song about the peace of life in the woods — to cheer us up, I suppose. The men finally decided that we could not reach home that night. Nobody was living in these woods; but Uncle John had noticed a little house by the roadside, where he hoped we could await daybreak. We had eaten a good snack before we left the train, so we needed no supper. Reaching the vacant house, of which the front door was open, we spread a large wagon sheet on the floor; and on it we rested more or less comfortably for the rest of the night. A fire had been kindled in the fireplace to light the room and to take away the dampness. The few quilts that had been folded on the seats of the hack were made into a pallet for Aunt Joline who was not used to such hardships. I took off an underskirt to wrap around the baby and used the handbag as a pillow. Of course the children slept soundly, but once in a while someone would sigh, "Oh, my bones." This was especially true of Aunt Joline.

With daybreak we started on our way—which was a slow procedure, for the road was very muddy. We arrived home about ten, anxious for a little breakfast. This return was certainly an adventure, but I enjoy thinking of it. The girls met us quite a distance from the house; they were so glad to have us back. They had looked for us ever since the night before. I might add that they had cooked peaches and rice for Father every day.

On Aunt Ida's Place

After moving back to Aunt Ida's place we lived there very contentedly for four more years. Aunt Ida had added two more rooms to the house. By papering the rooms the house was made attractive. In front of the gallery were six or seven large umbrella china with dense shade. We sat there in the summer time, especially after supper, and sang. I taught the children many songs and also how to carry different parts. They were soon very good at carrying the parts of a canon. Of this type of musical composition we soon knew quite a number. It was here on summer evenings that Father taught the children the different constellations and the names of the stars.

For Aunt Anna's wedding [to Bennie Fuchs, 1894] I took the smaller children and went to San Antonio for a week's visit. Annie and Ida stayed at home to do the housework for Father. At this time Father was county surveyor and often gone for several days. This happened while I was gone and just suited the girls. They would look after the chickens and attend to their other duties; and then go over to Uncle John's for a good time.

On January 12, 1896, we had another baby boy. This time we were surely at a loss for a name. Everybody thought of a different one. Aunt Joline said that we ought to name at least one child after a great musician. I mentioned that I had always liked the name Felix. Then she suggested that we name him after Felix Mendelssohn Bartholdi. This lengthy name we reduced to Felix Berthold, and everybody was satisfied. Grandfather Mackensen reminded us that Felix meant the Happy One. Little Felix was a very healthy child and always cheerful and contented. These characteristics have stayed with him; and to this day he is happy, healthy, cheerful and contented. He has his father's temperament.

When later—also at Aunt Ida's place—we had another little boy [August 24, 1898], I again suggested the name Julius, but Father again objected. So we called the boy Louis after Uncle Louis, but added the second name Dente after Father whose nickname this had been at home during his boyhood years. Because he was the only one in the family born in America and therefore could become president, the family called him President or Dente for short. Little Louis had the Mackensen temperament. He and Felix were always the best of companions. When Louis was four months old, we moved once more—this time to the old home in Bell County, and that is another story.

We Move to Bell County

Perhaps you will wonder why we left the Romberg community where we spent so many happy years with such good people. We had always hoped to live again on a place we owned. Such a home we could buy only in case we sold the ranch, but selling the ranch was a problem. Then our children were growing up and needed more schooling, and we did not want to send them away from home too young.

When Grandfather Mackensen gave each of his children some property, he asked whether we would be interested in taking the Bell County farm as it was not convenient for the other children to take it. We gladly consented and Father went up to investigate before we decided to move. He came back well pleased with the country and the method of farming. At that time much of the land around Holland was new; cotton produced well; and much grain, especially wheat, was raised. So we decided to move. However, we could not make the change until the tenants had vacated the house after Christmas.

About two weeks before Christmas Father started off to the new home with the wagon, two teams, and as many of the farming implements as he could take along. With him was a hired hand, Fritz Bauch. Just as he started off a norther blew up with snowflakes; but he decided to go anyway. The weather, however, got so bad that after a few miles he stopped with friends until it had moderated. Next morning the skies being clear, they proceeded and were on the road five days, driving through snow all the time. At night they stopped over in farm houses. The last night the only protection they could find was on the gallery of a Negro cabin. The last day Father did not stop for dinner or to feed his team because he was determined to reach the farm, where he arrived at four in the afternoon. For quite a while afterwards Father had trouble with his eyes, which was no doubt due to the glaring white of the snow and cold wind.

Father had wanted to make some preparations here before we arrived, but the weather was so severe that there was not much he could do.

In the meantime with the assistance of Grandfather Mackensen, we prepared for the moving. He did most of the packing, at which he was very good. Then we went over to Uncle John's house to spend the last week there to celebrate Christmas. Uncle John exerted himself to the utmost to make this one of the best Christmas celebrations that the children had ever had. Little Felix, three years old, was the one who admired the tree the most. He circled around it and repeated blissfully, "Pretty Christmas tree."

On the twenty-ninth of December, on my birthday, there was a farewell party. Our relatives and friends told us good-bye and expressed their good wishes. Next morning we had to be in La Grange early to take the train. Uncle John predicted another cold spell and was anxious to get his charges to the station before the norther would arrive. We got up early and rushed around to get everything packed. When dressing the children for the trip, we could not find Felix's shoes anywhere and finally he declared that he had packed them in one of the trunks. Of course the shoes could not be found, and he had to go without them. A cold norther struck us with full force when we were on the high bridge at La Grange. There was no time to buy another pair of shoes. People were astonished on that trip to see a little boy barefooted on so cold a day.

Our household goods had been shipped some days ahead by freight, and Father had intended to have them unloaded and in the house by the time we arrived. However, they were delayed. When we got off the train, Father was still busy unloading, and so he secured a hack and driver to take out the family. It was a curtained vehicle, but the roads were in bad condition after the heavy snow, and on the level stretches we got the full force of the norther. Finally we arrived at the empty cold house. The yard looked depressing. Deep ruts had been cut by the wheels of heavily loaded wagons as the folks moved out. The strong north wind had blown shucks and feed stalks over the yard. Everything looked uninviting except the floors, which had been scrubbed clean.

Our first work was to start a booming fire in the fireplace to get the babies warm. Father soon came up with the furniture, but it was too late to arrange it in the house, so that we all had to sleep on the floor on pallets that night. Little Erna, tired and sleepy, said, "Let's go home now."

Here we had the first New Year's evening without a celebration since we had been married.

We Establish Ourselves at the Cottonwood Home

Father was much in favor of getting the children off to school right away for fear they would get homesick. It was much work in this cold weather to get the four children well fed, dressed and wrapped and provided with lunches to go to school in time, for they had to walk two miles to get there. Ida, Hermann, Frederica, and Carl attended. The latter was eight years old. After they had left I could look after my babies. Little Louis was only four months old. I am still surprised how well we got by and in what good health we all were that winter, which was one of the coldest we have had in Texas.

All that winter I never had time to arrange everything the way I wanted it, and there were a number of things that were never unpacked. Soon the neighbors came to visit us, and the few old acquaintances that were still living here called on us as soon as the road would permit.

Finally the beautiful Texas spring weather set in. Father was happy to start this new enterprise, real farming. It was the first time that all his energies had been put into farming. Even a farmer has lots to learn in a new locality. The farm had been badly neglected . There were lots of weeds and poor fences. What Father wanted most were several good implements; and when the money from the first crop came in we invested in a drill, a cassady plow and a few other necessary implements instead of the buggy that we also needed.

The house also was much in need of improvements. The girls and I looked after that as best as we could with whitewash and wallpaper, with flowers and vines. We needed more room badly and about two years after our arrival we decided to build at least part of a new house. It is needless to say how much we enjoyed this new house with all its space.

Social life here was very different from what we had had in Fayette County, but we soon learned to feel at home. We had good and kind neighbors and plenty of visiting. Social activities consisted of going to church, attending singings and going to parties. As we intended to live among these people, we tried to fit into this new environment. We had the only piano in the neighborhood, but there were a few organs.

One afternoon in the spring Father came in to announce that some of the young men in the neighborhood had asked him for permission to have a party at our house, and that he had given his consent. I could not see how we could give a party in our small house filled up with furniture, but Father said we could not get out of it now because the young men had already started up the hills to announce the party. By moving some of the furniture out of the front room, we provided enough space.

It certainly was a party! The gallery, front room and bedroom were crowded. This country was full of young people at that time. We had the problem of how to entertain. Father got out his violin and played some songs which one of the girls accompanied on the piano, and the girls played some duets. Finally we found out that they enjoyed games. In these we were experienced, since we had played a great many different games of this sort in the Romberg community. When our guests finally departed we had the satisfied feeling of having given them a pleasant evening. Later, especially after we had more room, we gave many a party here. Young people have to have amusement. It appealed more to us to give entertainments for the children in our home where we could be with them than to have them seek pleasures outside of their home. Social gatherings in the homes, parties, were popular at that time.

When Father let it be known that he was willing to survey again, he got lots of work. He enjoyed its and it brought in a nice extra income. Much land was bought and sold here then as prices for farms were steadily going up. The old Goode farm of five thousand acres just south of us was gradually subdivided and sold. As there was much work on the farm and the children were too young to be of much assistance, we had to have hired help for a number of years.

As Father was anxious to make more than the farm would produce, he got interested in a thresher. First he managed this enterprise with two partners; later he owned one by himself. A thresher brought a good income, but it caused also much work and worry. During the threshing season, Father left home very early and came home late, even though he had a very good threshing crew. He paid his men well and treated them well, and all of them were anxious to work for him year after year. Working with the engine probably stimulated Carl to take up engineering when he went to college.

During all this Father continued to make improvements on the farm. He fenced it in in such a way that it could be well pastured in different seasons. One worry was how to control the surplus water during heavy rains. If at that time we could have had the soil conservation service, Father would have taken a great interest in it and would have cooperated gladly. Some of the measures that are advocated by that service now, for conserving and improving the fertility of the soil, he employed long ago.

The pleasantest thing on the farm to me was a beautiful spring with so much clear water, all running down the creek.

One of the first improvements I hoped for was running water in my kitchen. At first such an expense could
not be thought of. But Father knew of the use of a hy-
draulic ram, and one day he happened to meet a man in
Belton who could give exact information on how to mea-
sure the flow of the water and how to select the suitable
size of pump. So it was not long before we had the
pump and a cistern of good size. With running water in
the kitchen and a sink, I enjoyed conveniences I had
wanted for a long time.

Our spring is now not as strong as it was at that time,
for the branch has washed out and new springs have
formed farther up in the branch.

It was years later before we had a spring house built.
This was done by Carl. Our spring house has been in-
valuable to keep our large supply of milk, butter and
lots of things that had to be kept cool in summer. No one
enjoyed the convenience of an ice box then.

One of Father's hobbies was planting trees. Our
house was away from the grove in the hot sunshine. The
second winter Father planted a half dozen hackberry
trees around the house and ordered some peach trees,
which he planted in a long row up the field south of the
house. These trees got to be beautiful trees and supplied
us for years with lots of luscious fruit. He also planted
pears in an orchard west of the house. These had beautiful large red-cheeked pears, of which Conrad once ex-
hibited some at the Belton fair and won a prize. After a
few years these trees all died of root rot, and only the
few planted in the grove remained. These we still have,
and they still bear well.

When we moved back here there were in this grove
still a few pecan trees that had been here in my childhood days, so I was convinced that pecans would do
well. I decided that we might as well have them in the
grove as the hackberry trees; so I planted nuts all over

the grove the very first winter. Of course it took years for a few of them to grow up. At that time the Dallas Semi-Weekly News brought articles about pecan culture with illustrations as to how to bud and improve them. I was much interested in this and saved the articles, hoping that we might try this new method some day. Louis was the one who finally took great interest in this work and budded these trees. Now we are proud of the nice pecan grove in our yard — after forty years.

Carl was always planning how to make a little spare money. When he was about fifteen, he helped Mr. Thornhill to rob bees and bought two stands from him, which were moved here next winter. Since then we have always had bees on this place. Later when Carl was off at college, Felix and Father looked after the bees.

Like a great many old places throughout Texas, this one had bois d'arc hedges. These hedges had been planted with the hope of making good enclosures against cattle in the prairies where it was difficult and expensive to get enough rails for fences. However, the plan proved unsuccessful; for some of the trees got root rot causing big gaps in the hedges. On our farm these hedges had spread and took up some of the very best land. Besides they ran right through the fields, and so they were a general nuisance. Father was determined to have them removed. He was lucky to find a man who was willing to undertake this job, which took months. Finally the land was all cleared and put under cultivation. But we were not rid of these bois d'arcs yet. Numerous sprouts came up. On a set day each week Father went over the land and systematically destroyed the sprouts. And so he succeeded in getting entirely rid of the bois d'arcs, and recovered acres of the best soil on the farm.

Not every one of our undertakings on this farm turned out a success. We always had many chickens on this farm, since the place is well suited with its shade and running water. We brought several coops of brown leghorn chickens along from Fayette County. We had thought that ducks would do well here, and so Father one day bought some from a peddler in town and brought them proudly home. Was I astonished when I saw four drakes and one duck! Father had selected these fowls for their attractive plumage. The ducks thrived, were easy to raise and good to eat. We served many a duck. However, they would wander off down the creek and spend their days with neighbors that fed them with watermelons in the summer; and finally the ducks dispensed with the trouble of coming home at night. We had to get rid of them. Then some time later Father brought home two big geese and one gander, thinking they would be an asset to the farm. However, these senseless geese insisted on spending the night on the gravel in front of our porch chattering with each other on moonlight nights. Before daybreak they would be back in the spring bathing; then when the team was brought to the trough, the water was full of feathers. So it was decided to sell the geese to Mrs. Gray, our neighbor. We succeeded in raising one gosling to which little Felix was especially attached and which he had named Munulate. I remember well how distressed he was when Mrs. Gray came for the geese and how he begged with tears in his eyes that we keep Munulate. I consoled him by explaining that the little gosling would love to stay with his mother, that Mrs. Gray would take very good care of him, that we would go and see him, and so on.

We then tried turkeys, and with these we had success. We raised as many as 75 or 100 at times. They were very little work, and the income from them was good. I certainly enjoyed raising the little turkeys. They got so gentle and thrived so. The most work connected with them came in spring when the turkey hens wandered down to the creek to hide their nests. Hunting these nests and bringing in the eggs was suitable and pleasant work for the children. No one could trail a wary hen better than Felix, who slipped after her secretly like an Indian after quail. He was also good for setting traps for the pole cats and opossums that also were anxious to get the turkey eggs.

Pranks and Plays at Cottonwood Home

O ur place could be recognized from the distance by the two enormous cottonwood trees in the back yard. It took three men, stand standing up, to reach around the trunk. These trees were already large in my childhood. We children called them after our brothers. The larger one, the Bernhard tree, seemed to lean to the south; and when the north wind was blowing strong, we children used to race along the trail that led underneath, for fear the tree might tumble over.

When I returned after a generation to live here again, the two trees were still a distinctive feature of our place, so we called the place the Cottonwood Home.

The summer when Erich Perlitz was here to build the second part of our house, he went up to the top of the Bernhard cottonwood by climbing first up a hackberry tree and then over a grapevine to the first big branch of the cottonwood. He claimed that the view from up there was fine. A few days later Conrad, then about nine, perched on the first limb of that cottonwood, having tried the same route. But he could not get back down. He was in a precarious position, and no ladder could reach him. Cousin Erich helped him down. How it was done I do not know, for I did not look on.

Those two big trees that must have been a century old are gone now. One was struck by lightning, and the other suffered so much during a three years' drought culminating in 1918 that large branches were later dry and began to drop off. The tree was so close to the house that the children were always passing below or playing there. It was impossible to attempt to saw off large limbs at such great height, and so after much deliberation we decided it would be best to cut down the entire tree. We consoled ourselves with the thought that it would be more useful to have a pecan growing in its place.

I should have mentioned that when Conrad was born in 1902 [September 25,1902], I again wished to call the boy Julius. This time I had the advantage of having the girls on my side. Father objected to the name as he had done before; and when Grandfather suggested Conrad, Father consistently called him by that name, while we women folks called him Julius. To avoid confusion for the little fellow, we finally called him Conrad Julius.

He was naturally everybody's pet, and maybe for that reason we decided — especially the grown children — not to spoil him, as is so often the case with the youngest child in a large family. We found out gradually that it was utterly impossible to spoil him. It was not in his nature to be spoiled.

It was Father's idea that the children should have a swimming hole; and in order to have it, a dam had to be built across the creek. He selected a place north of the house that was completely shaded and conveniently near. The dam was so well built that it remained for many years — till the boys were grown and away from home. During the long summer season the swimming hole was in daily use and gave lots of pleasure. All of the children learned how to swim. As the place was perfectly private, we womenfolks went bathing in the afternoons, attired in discarded dresses or in more up-to-date short-skirted and short-sleeved swimming suits made of old woolen garments.

The boys added such refinements as a diving board and a boat to the place.

The first attempts at boat building were not successful. The one Felix built was soon used as a feed trough in the lot. Carl built his of tin, but it was so light that it always turned over. Later on the hired man built one that was anchored in the creek when not in use for a longer time. The swimming hole extended quite a piece up the creek so that with the use of some imagination a nice boat trip could be taken.

The boys were not hampered with suits. The undressing was done on the run, and when they reached the swimming hole they were ready to dive in. They were not permitted to stay in too long. If they did so, they forfeited their swim the next day. This was a private swimming place. Father did not permit outsiders to make use of it.

I Develop Some Wrinkles and Gray Hairs

Life in a large family is not always filled with pleasure. It does not always run along quietly and peacefully in an even tenor. Off and on there will be a sudden scare or a prolonged worry. After these, one can appreciate the happy days.

Fortunately my family was in good health. I think this was partly due to the fact that we had plenty of plain and well-prepared food and enough rest at night. It happened very seldom that we took the children out at night. Ordinarily they had to go to bed regularly at an early hour so that they got plenty of sleep. We had large bedrooms, single beds and plenty of fresh air.

With so many boys in the house and with woods along both of our creeks, it was natural that hunting should become a major sport. At first hunting was done with dogs and traps. When Carl was old enough to use a target, Grandfather gave the boys such a gun. This made hunting more successful and also more dangerous. Father said the boys had to learn how to handle a gun, and he taught them every precaution.

Of course when Carl got older, the target was not sufficient for his needs; and so he got a shotgun. I believe it was a repeater. The place for these guns was on beams in the kitchen where they were out of reach of small children. One day when Conrad and I were in the kitchen, Father came in and got down the repeater; and while examining it, the gun went off with a loud explosion. This gave Father and me a terrible shock. We could not help thinking that Conrad could have been hurt. It was amazing that this sort of an accident should have happened to

Father who was always so very careful. We found later that the gun was not quite reliable and got rid of it.

One Sunday morning Felix left with the target to hunt a bit down in the creek, as he would often do. There was always that old crow that cried derisively from the top of the limb of the highest tree and outwitted the boys on every occasion. This time Felix did not come back in time. Finally it got to be dinner time, and still no Felix. Afternoon. Felix still gone. I got awfully nervous, because this had never happened before. I telephoned to several neighbors and asked whether they had seen my boy. I was so upset that I told Father when the boy turned up he needed a good punishment, that it was all wrong to stay away without permission this way. Later someone telephoned us that Felix and Ben Hurst had been seen going up the road to Hackberry. It was some relief to know that he was not alone, but still I declared he needed punishment. When we were at the supper table Felix came in so tired out that he was almost in tears. They had jumped twenty-two jackrabbits in one volunteer oat patch; the dogs finally would not even chase them anymore. The one Felix shot he carried a long way to bring back to me; but finally when the rabbit got too heavy or the boy too tired, he left it behind. I was so relieved to have my boy back home again safe that the punishment was forgotten. But leaving home for such a length of time without permission was not done anymore.

A few times I was thoroughly frightened because a horse—even a tame one—would occasionally run away with the buggy and the drivers. When Carl and Frederica returned from school in the buckboard one day, they carelessly dropped the reins when coming through the gate up the road. When they tried to pick the reins up with the help of the whip, gentle old Gray got scared and ran away. I heard a commotion and saw the horse dashing across the bridge and around the barns down into the pasture with only Carl in the seat of the vehicle. When the frightened horse turned a sharp corner, Carl was thrown off into some bushes. And where was Frederica? She had climbed off the back of the buckboard and came screaming after. This time the scare was the worst part of the experience.

Another time Louis was in a runaway. He was then a boy of about twelve years. Threshing was going on in the fields south of the house. In the buckboard he was carrying drinking water to the men when Toby took a sudden notion that the setting was perfect for a runaway. The first thing I saw was a streak of Toby with the empty buckboard going across the front yard. He stopped abruptly at the hay stack and started nibbling after this spree. Then I saw Father coming towards the house carrying Louis on his back. The boy was moaning and his face was bloody. I have never felt more relieved than when the doctor, who came soon, declared that he could find nothing seriously the matter. But to this day Louis claims that he has a small dent in his head that he received from his fall against the wheel.

One Sunday Carl and his friend Mack used a long rope to make a particularly high swing. Next morning the rope was still swinging from the limb; and Father told Carl to take it down, as it was needed. From the breakfast table I could see how quickly Carl climbed up the rope and unfastened it. All at once the rope began to slip and down came Carl, landing with a whack on his side in the dust. I was there when he started whimpering pitifully and was sure he was badly injured. He was badly shaken up but got by without injury.

This is enough of this harrowing subject. Of course there were other smaller happenings, such as taking a tumble off the bicycle and stepping on nails. The whooping cough was not bad; and during the days when the children were shut up with measles, they engaged in wagers as to who would have the reddest skin next morning.

All of these experiences contributed to my gray hair and to the wrinkles in my face. I am glad that a good many of my wrinkles are the results of happy smiles, also caused by the children.

The Children Get Rich

I would like to have a cheerful subject after the last topic, so I will tell you how the children got rich — at least in their own estimation.

Father and I always thought it a good plan for the children to earn a little money and to learn how to spend it in a way that would bring them the greatest enjoyment. We gave them an opportunity to earn a little here and there. The small amount they received was really laughable. But it is not the amount they got but the satisfaction of having something that belonged to them through their own efforts that made money valuable. They were to learn to make a small income go a long way. Besides we were not financially in a position to spend much in this manner, for there were many children whom we were anxious to give a good schooling. This schooling could not be accomplished without plenty of money.

The children had different sources for their income. Cotton picking perhaps brought in most funds, especially if they could pick for the neighbors a few days. The honey and the vegetables they had to sell and that I would buy, brought in further funds. Then there was the lucrative business of gathering the eggs for a nickel per hundred eggs. And there was income from other similar jobs.

When it came to spending the money, the mail-order houses were patronized mostly. The catalogs were very carefully studied, the items were selected and written down. This list was then revised so that some money would be left for future grants. A peculiarity of the items selected was that they were mostly presents for Christmas. A number of these little items were bought for two to five cents; but they were practical and suitable, and gave as much joy to the giver as an expensive gift would have done. No one was forgotten. It was valuable training for the children to select with forethought these little items.

A larger financial venture was undertaken when Father assisted the children to buy from a tenant some unpicked cotton left in the field. From this venture the children realized thirty dollars. Of curse the big question was how the money should be spent. When Father suggested buying an Edison phonograph, the children were overjoyed. Father ordered the machine and a dozen records from the Edison factory in New Jersey. In due time the package arrived, was unpacked and set up. The big horn was attached, and the first record, "The Crown Diamond Overture," played by the London Military Band, was heard. All listened spellbound, for the music was unbelievably beautiful.

The children would hurry from school anxious to hear a little music first before doing their chores for the evening. Father and I thought that music had a refining and educational influence and that we could have such music only through this instrument. So Father decided to order four dozen more records, which I selected with much deliberation so that would not only get more pieces but also the right variety. Later a record was always a suitable birthday present. We were careful to keep the records in good condition so that we would not lose the beauty of their tone.

It was always a particular pleasure for the children to give a present to Father or to me—a grand one for Christmas. On one twenty-fourth of December, after dinner, the children were anxious to see me go upstairs to take a little afternoon rest. I easily suspected what was up and gave then the pleasure of keeping myself busy upstairs. I could not help hearing that there was much commotion below, and that the big wagon was driven up to the house. That night my best present was a kitchen cupboard that was presented to me with beaming eyes by my children.

Another Christmas Father was presented with a desk. This was hidden under a mysterious-looking covered heap in one corner of the room that afternoon. That night after the rest of the celebration was over, the children managed the climax of the evening to which they had been looking forward. With much enthusiasm they blindfolded Father and led him around in the room to confuse him and to gain time for uncovering the desk and for placing the new desk chair at just the right angle. Finally Father was seated before the desk and the bandage was taken off. He was surely surprised and pleased to see this long needed piece of furniture. It takes the father of many children to play his part just right on such an important occasion. This present was one of the most useful presents Father ever got and will serve for many more years.

Another time, it was on our wedding day I think, the children got up a special celebration in the big room where we parents had to sit in state, before a strange-looking covered-up piece of furniture. The children proceeded with a program of homemade verses appropriate for the occasion, and finally at the right moment the cover was removed—and we were presented with a red plush sofa. This time the grown girls away from home had been approached for contributions by the instigators at home.

The cupboard is still in good use. However, it changes its color occasionally. But the old sofa has had a hard time in its life, especially after the grandchildren romped over it for years, causing it to lose its elasticity and to get bumpy. We finally decided that it had had its day; and so it was removed up to my bedroom where it can still be of use, when unfolded, as a bed in time of many visitors. At other times the old sofa with its many associations reminds me of the many happy days spent when it was still in use downstairs and in the center of our happy family life. When I think of those days I think they brought me happiness and joy with so many healthy and energetic children around us. To me the gift and the pleasure with which it was given showed that although there was no luxury and wealth in our home, the children loved their parents and their home and were happy in it.

My Four Daughters

I was very proud of my four little girls, for they were sweet, pretty and helpful. They were all somewhat different. Annie was lively, playful and full of pranks; Ida more quiet, industrious and dependable. Frederica was an especially gifted child. She was really good at every task around the house. Erna was always even-tempered and in a good humor. She was easily managed; she was petted a good deal but was not the type to be easily spoiled.

Annie was very kindhearted and just loved to give, which she does to this day. Her Aunt Joline told me one time that I must keep an eye on this trait or some day she would give away the clothes on her back. She was talkative, was a bookworm and had splendid musical talent. She was not so suited for housework. Having had an older brother as a playmate for years, she was always on the best terms with the boy cousins that grew up with her.

Ida loved her dolls and was mighty good in helping around the house. She was industrious and dependable and good to look after the children. Since these two girls were the oldest children, they had lots of duties and were a great help to me. I enjoyed sewing for them and keeping them in neat and becoming clothing.

Frederica and Hermann were always the best of pals. As a baby Frederica was mostly taken for a boy instead of a girl, and Father saw much resemblance with his mother in features and stature. She was a great help to me when the older girls left home early. She took an interest in all the different types of housework and did such work especially well.

There was never so much work expected of Erna. Perhaps because the older sisters were around. In many ways Erna had the advantage over her sisters. For instance, she had two older brothers who were always willing to take her out to parties and dances and other social affairs. She was plentifully supplied with nice clothes that her grown sisters helped to provide. Because she had older sisters and brothers, she started early to attend social affairs, and it became easy for her to meet people. It was a pleasure to see how thoroughly she could enjoy herself.

All four girls loved music and learned to play the piano. They liked their school work and were good students.

Grandfather

I have mentioned the good influence that the relatives in the Romberg community, especially the kind and capable aunts, had on our family. A very definite influence came also from Grandfather Mackensen.

When we moved to Cottonwood Home, Grandfather spent the summers with us; and when we planned the new house, we saw to it that Grandfather got a quiet, suitable room, where he could retire whenever he desired. To this day the room is still called Grandfather's room.

It was always a joy when Grandfather arrived, for everybody loved him. He brought with him an antique valise and a small trunk, which contained all his necessities. The trunk was mostly filled with a light featherbed, taken along to hold the rest of the contents in place. Like the philosopher Diogenes, Grandfather was contented with very few belongings. He said he did not want to be hampered with too many possessions. The trunk contained a few everyday clothes, his many pipes, pipestems and various tobaccos; a few early photographs of his family; a well bound book in which he kept his accounts; and the book of logarithms that he had used when in the navigation school in Bremen. He and Father made up problems that they would present one to the other for solution. For such purposes that book of logarithms was still used.

Grandfather had good health, was cheerful and contented and very careful not to be any trouble to anybody. He was loving and affectionate and very much devoted to his family. He never found fault or criticized any member of his family, although he could criticize impersonal affairs such as national policies.

He came out for breakfast when the morning rush was over. It was my habit to be at the table then for a pleasant chat while he was eating breakfast. After that he had a smoke and read a while in his room. As long as he could, he liked to do something about the place every morning. After noon, he took a nap and again appeared later in the afternoon. Then I saw to it that he had something to drink, coffee or lemonade, and some cookies, often ginger cookies. That was a good time to visit with him — usually on the porch. Later on he might read some more, for he was a great reader. His light evening meal he ate early. At night Father often read to him or the two talked together.

Grandfather had a great deal of will power and a very high sense of honor. For him there was no compromise between right and wrong. He had excellent judgment, and Father and I often asked his opinion and followed his advice in business and other problems.

Although he had had many reverses in life, he stayed cheerful. One tragedy in his life was that my mother at the age of fifty-four after a severe illness lost her power of speech for a period of ten years. When this faculty seemed to return, she died suddenly of a minor malady. Another tragedy in Grandfather's life was the loss of two of his children when they were still in their best years. First Aunt Annie died and then Uncle Bernhard.

Grandfather was softhearted, and he had a strong temper. This temper was inherited by me and brother Louis, by sons Carl and Louis. The other children have Father's equanimity, his peaceful mood. Grandfather could laugh easily, and tears also came easily. He enjoyed music and liked to sing even in his old age. For a long time he kept his good voice. When the girls practiced at the piano, he would frequently hum or sing the melody. Often he was not conscious of doing this. He liked tragic music.

Grandfather brought a great deal of entertainment into the house. It was never difficult to keep up a good conversation when he was in our home, for he had a good education, had traveled a great deal, was well informed and had an excellent memory. Besides he had a long life of rich experiences, a life that began in a European village where medieval conditions still prevailed, took him through pioneer times in Texas and finally included life in modern cities. It was a sign of sane living and thinking that he lived to be 103 years old.

When Grandfather and Father were engaged in a discussion which was usually based on national or international affairs, I saw to it that there was no disturbance. He could tell anecdotes and stories well. Of these he had an inexhaustible supply. Everybody in the family enjoyed them. And he could laugh heartily about his humorous stories himself.

Very enjoyable for the children were the summer nights when the boys lay stretched out on the lawn in front of the house and listened to Grandfather and other grown folks talking. What the children hear in this manner around fireplace and at the family table makes a deep impression and influences their thinking and their character.

In Conclusion

You will see from this narrative how different the life of pioneer children was. We were deprived of so many conveniences and so much entertainment that you have now; but you must not think that the pioneer children were not happy, for we did not know a different life and did not miss it. We were perfectly contented with what we had. We found entertainment and enjoyment mostly through our more intimate contacts with nature, with plants and all sorts of little creatures.

As time went on and the newer inventions and conveniences came into our life, they were received with astonishment and admiration. The railroad, the telephone, the phonograph, the automobile and finally the airplane —all these things were new to us; and we gradually got acquainted with them. Now these improvements that were wonders to us are taken for granted, for they have become a part of everyday life. The children of today, therefore, miss the pleasure and excitement that come with such progress. Of course there are inventions and improvements now, but these in our present full life do not make the deep impression nor do they change as much our mode of living as the earlier ones did.

We often hear old people speak of the good old times when life was easy and unpretentious. There is much to that viewpoint. For the very conveniences of modern life also bring with them problems and difficulties. Now it is a problem for conscientious parents not to surround their children with too much ease, not to indulge and spoil them—of which there is danger now—but to keep them wholesomely occupied. In pioneer days our time and our thoughts were not scattered and dissipated with too many different activities. We had leisure to absorb

the influences with which we came in contact. The influences that shaped our thinking were more under control
than they are now, for we had more home life at that
time. Of course Father and I were fortunate to have parents who had the knowledge and ability and the desire
to enrich and direct our lives.

It is time to close this narrative. When you are reading it I hope you will enjoy once more your happy childhood and the people connected with it, the foremost of
whom was your unselfish father, whose greatest wish
was that his children should be well brought up and
well prepared to live a good life. They were his absorbing interest. When other people invested their money to
accumulate more wealth, he invested his savings in the
education of his children. And we have been well
pleased with the outcome — now that we have seen how
well you have succeeded in life.

Cottonwood Home

by

Erna Romberg Bartels

After a morning of housework
Of cooking and working with chickens,
Resting, I sit in a rocker
Enjoying the peace of the evening.
Helen and Linda are playing,
Are making some cookies, some mudpies.
Seeing them busily playing
Reminds me of days of my childhood.
Under a bois d'arc's arches
I'm playing with Felix and Luttie.
March wind is swaying the tree tops.
Their newly grown leaflets are dainty.
About me in changing patterns
Their shadow I see on the ground.
Flowers are blooming around us.
A humming of bees I am hearing.
Redbirds are singing their cheery
"It's springtime, it's springtime, it's spring."

Now all at once it is summer.
Some cousins have come on a visit.
Talking and laughing and musing
We gather about the veranda.
Grandfather, cheerfully smoking,
Reclines in the cushioned rocker.
Annie is reading a booklet.
My mother is mending our clothes.
Felix, a generous talker,
Enlivens a game of checkers.
Hermann's sonorous singing

Is drowning the phonograph's music.
Ida is snapping a picture
Of Otto holding the kitty.
Out on the lawn of bermuda
The boys are tumbling and wrestling,
Scaring the turkeys that loiter
Under the pomegranate bushes.

The season now changes to autumn.
The cotton has nearly been gathered.
Sunday has come. We are strolling
To gather some native pecans.
The grown-ups are crossing the footlog.
We children are wading instead.
The creek-bed is covered with pebbles,
Some minnows are darting to cover.
Carl has a gun and is hoping
That Watchie will scare up a rabbit.
Berries and flowers we gather,
And slide down the steepest of creek banks.
Slowly the sun is setting
Behind the towering cottonwoods.
Homeward we trudge with our treasures,
Wasp nests and rocks and flowers.
Hungry I go to the kitchen
To help with the serving of supper.

Now it is winter. It sleeted.
The grove is sparkling with jewels.
Wind is shaking the tree tops.
The ice-covered branches are crackling.
Huddled in wraps I am running
To get from the spring house some water.
Trying to skate on the bridge
I loiter a while at the spring branch.
Cold is urging me homeward,
So into the kitchen I hurry.
Hermann before the fireplace
Is poking the fire and mumbling.

Father beside a window
Is reading the Literary Digest.
Mother, while mending a stocking,
Is telling a story to Conrad.
Comfort is here and contentment
In the heart of Cottonwood Home.

On Having Five Brothers

Written for Mother's Day by Annie Romberg

When I look back on my experiences with my five younger brothers, I have the impression that the day began regularly with the efforts of getting Carl out of bed in time for breakfast. Always very effective in arousing the sleeper were the efforts of the other brothers still upstairs—judging from the tumult stirred up. Also effective and picturesque was such a device as a string of cow bells and tin cans suspended well out of reach above Carl's bed and operated by means of twine and wire from the head of the stairs, from which vantage place a safe escape could always be made when the thoroughly aroused and irate Carl suddenly appeared, half clad, to put a stop to the racket.

After breakfast, I usually tied up a sore big toe, and then started house cleaning with all its problems. The boys had won out in the endurance test concerning the baseball outfit. One stepped over balls and bats on the porch and swept around them in the hall. When visitors arrived, one could take a mitt, large as a milk pan, off the sofa and say, "Boys are funny, aren't they?" Mother approved of my attitude regarding the baseball necessities, but she omitted the remark about boys being funny. A bat never leans against a tree or a wall. It always sprawls on the ground, impeding progress.

Handling the collection of rocks and shells, when cleaning up the house, was easy. So many specimens decorated the mantle piece and filled the sewing machine drawers and mother's vases, that a few could always be removed without arousing objections. The difference in quantity would not be noticeable; besides, the supply would continually be replenished with new rare pieces.

The picture Conrad drew in the third grade, which had found a place on the wall right over the piano — through the hands of the artist himself probably and probably with Mother's permission — required more experience and diplomacy. The best system was to drop it behind the piano for a while. If it was missed, it could always be found and replaced. One had to look innocent and sympathetic on occasions like that.

The big wasp nest that Felix brought in only a few days ago and hung conveniently over the picture of great-grandmother, hiding that worthy lady's imposing-looking cap almost entirely, of course, had to be respected for another week or two. Its ultimate removal to the museum upstairs, known as the boys' room, required careful preliminary maneuvering.

The twig with five pecans in one bunch, which Louis presented to Father and which was pinned to the window curtain by Father's desk, would have to remain indefinitely. Mother had made it plain that it must be respected, even though it collected dust. Perhaps some day one of the boys would bring home a bride, and in the excitement of getting the house ready for the arrival, that bunch might be swept away with a number of other similar specimens.

Sometime in the middle of the day the question would arise: "Does anybody know whether the boys have fed the pet rabbit?" The prevailing idea among the elders was that the care of pets taught responsibility. While such necessary and useful domestic animals as cats and dogs were, however, exempted from the care of the boys, other occasional pets were supposedly left entirely under their guardianship. Most of the pets had short lives. The rabbit was housed in an elaborate apartment that was added to and diversified each free afternoon. The feeding and watering were mostly forgotten. I finally set him free. To this day, when the subject of the pet rabbit comes up, I am accused of heartlessness — to the boys, not the rabbit.

The pet coon was discouraging. He slept all day. Not even when he was displayed to guests would he respond as much as to open even one eye. Besides, he smelled disagreeably. The pet owl was not much better. She was permitted to roost in the boys' room all day, and left by the open window in the evening. The roosting had its undesirable features. I discouraged the owl until she finally stayed away. Although my negotiations with her were carried on with the utmost secrecy, Hermann immediately accused me of lack of hospitality. She was fed with earthworms, dug up by the hour.

The pet spider on the porch ceiling was a glutton and fattened visibly under the attentions of the boys, who brought larger and larger prey and engaged in wagers as to which of the two animals would win in each struggle.

The noon meal of the family was regularly delayed because bathing in the swimming hole preceded. The established method of recalling the boys was to beat the plowshare suspended for this purpose from the hackberry tree near the kitchen door. If this blinding and staggering din did not bring the boys, one followed the path towards the swimming hole, passing first straw hats, then shirts, and finally overalls, inverted. One stopped at the last overall and waved it at the first slick head appearing above the bushes. The waving was effective. It meant the law of the land — Mother.

It was amazing that the boys would stay in swimming so long when they were near starvation — as was evident when they did reach the dinner table. The usual method to prevent an utter collapse was to seize the dish nearest the plate, take a generous helping, and begin to eat immediately. A boy, however, can reach a rubber-like arm easily to all parts of a large family table without in-convenience. If not interfered with, he can eat meat and potatoes in one part of his mouth, and pie in another, lift up a spoonful of gravy with one hand, a glass of milk with the other, and ask for the butter—all at the same time—if not interfered with.

The conversation at the table could have consisted of a continued series of statements each one beginning with "Don't." Mother's system was to encourage Father and Grandfather to continue an interesting conversation concerning the Boer war or the Non-partisan League, or something like that, and to keep well-filled dishes circu-lating in the direction of the boys.

The conversation of the boys in those days, if my memory is correct, consisted chiefly of stating more rea-sons why another fishing trip to the river should be un-dertaken. Whole weeks, it seems to me, were spent in making promises regarding rules of health and safety that were to be observed on the next trip.

Speaking of eating. Bread and butter was permitted in the middle of the long summer afternoon—under cer-tain restrictions. Almost any afternoon, when there were suspicious whisperings and a prolonged stay in the kitchen ending upon my approach with the slamming of the kitchen cupboard door and the creak of the back screen door, I would find the restrictions not properly observed. Crumbs everywhere. The bread knife, smeared to the handle with butter and honey, leaning greasily against the sugar bowl. Drippings from the di-rection of the meat dish would indicate that it, too, had been invaded. Well, as long as Mother overlooked it.

After supper usually bed and slumber without delay. It is strange how in sleep the features of the most impish boy will assume an angelic expression. Probably this fact explains why Mother had so much patience with those five lively brothers of mine.

CPSIA information can be obtained
at www.ICGtesting.com
Printed in the USA
BVHW031607221120
R11503600001B/R115036PG592846BVX5B/5